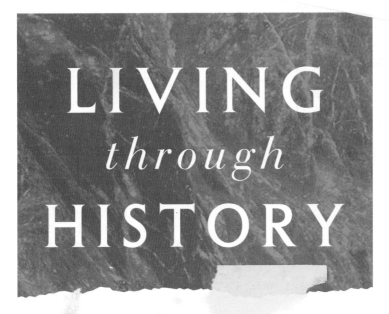

LIVING *through* HISTORY

the Roman Empire

Nigel Kelly, Rosemary Rees
and Jane Shuter

Heinemann

Acknowledgements

The authors and publishers would like to thank the following for permission to reproduce photographs:

Ancient Art & Architecture Collection: 1.1A, 1.1B, 5.1C, 8.1B
Bridgeman Art Library/Tabley House, University of Manchester: 5.1A
British Museum: 1.2B, p52, 6.5A, 6.6C
Brookside Productions: 1.4A
University of Cambridge/Aerial photography collection: 7.2B
Colchester Museums: 3.1D
C.M. Dixon: 2.1A, 3.3B, 6.6A
Robert Estall Photo Library/Malcolm Aird: 7.3C
Michael Holford: 4.1A, 4.1B
A K Kersting: 8.1A
Kobal Collection/MGM: 6.2A
Rex Features: 1.4B
Scala/Galleria Borghese, Rome: 6.2C
Scala/Museo della Ciuilta Romana, Rome: 6.1B
Society of Antiquaries of London: 3.2A
Edwin Smith: 5.1E
The National Trust Photographic Library/ Ian Shaw: 6.4B
Werner Forman Archive: 5.1C
York Archaeological Trust: 1.4A

The publishers have made every effort to trace copyright holders of material in this book. Any omissions will be rectified in subsequent printings if notice is given to the publisher.

The publishers would like to thank Dr Peter Heather for his comments on the original manuscript.

The authors and publishers gratefully acknowledge the following publications from which written sources in the book are drawn. In some sources the wording or sentence structure has been simplified.

A Bowman, *Life and Letters on the Roman Frontier*, British Museum Press, 1994: 3.3C, 7.5F
Julius Caesar, *The Conquest of Gaul*, trans. S A Handford, Penguin, 1982: 7.1B
F R Conwell, *Everyday Life in Ancient Rome*, B T Batsford, 1963: 6.4C, 6.4D
Cassius Dio, *Roman History*, trans. E Cary, Harvard UP, 1925: 7.3B
C Greig, Pliny: *A Selection of his Letters*, CUP, 1978: 5.1B, 6.2B
The *Guardian*, 16th January, 1997: 6.5B
Josephus, *The Jewish War*, ed. E M Smallwood, Penguin, 1981: 3.1C

Livy, *The Early History of Rome*, trans. A De Selincourt, Penguin, 1969: 2.2A
R D MacNaughten (trans.), *Rome, its People, Life and Customs*, McKay, 1963: 6.1C
Martial, *The Twelve Books of Epigrams*, trans. J A Pott and F A Wright, Dutton, 1924: 6.4E
R Nichols and K McLeith, *Through Roman Eyes*, OUP, 1976: 6.1A, 6.2D, 6.6B
QED – The Body in the Bog, BBC Television, 1985: 1.2D, 1.2E
The Sunday Times magazine, 6th April, 1997: 1.2C
Gaius Suetonius Tranquillus, *The Twelve Caesars*, trans. R Graves, The Folio Society, 1957: 1.1C
Tacitus, *The Imperial Annals of Rome*, trans. M Grant, Penguin, 1973: 3.1A, 7.2A, 7.3D, 7.3E
The Times, 26th September, 1996: 3.3C
J Wilkes, *The Roman Army*, CUP, 1972: 3.3A

First published in Great Britain by Heinemann Library, Halley Court, Jordan Hill, Oxford OX2 8EJ, a division of Reed Educational and Professional Publishing Ltd

OXFORD FLORENCE PRAGUE MADRID ATHENS MELBOURNE AUCKLAND KUALA LUMPUR SINGAPORE TOKYO IBADAN NAIROBI KAMPALA JOHANNESBURG GABORONE PORTSMOUTH NH (USA) CHICAGO MEXICO CITY SAO PAULO

First published 1997

01 00 99
10 9 8 7 6 5 4 3 2 1

British Library Cataloguing in Publication Data
Kelly, Nigel, 1954 –
    The Roman Empire. – (Living through history)
    1.Rome – History – Empire, 30 BC – 476 AD – Juvenile literature
    I.Title II.Rees, Rosemary, 1942– III.Shuter, Jane
    937'.06

ISBN 0 431 07195 0 hardback
ISBN 0 431 07193 4 paperback

Designed and produced by Dennis Fairey and Associates Ltd

Illustrated by Richard Berridge, Finbarr O' Connor, John James, Angus McBride, Arthur Phillips, Piers Sanford and Stephen Wisdom.

Printed in Spain by Edelvives

Cover design by Wooden Ark

CONTENTS

How do we know about the Romans?

The Romans lived thousands of years ago. Roman historians say the city of Rome was built nearly 800 years before Christ was born. It is very difficult to find out about people who lived so long ago. Most of their buildings have been replaced. Many of their belongings have rotted away.

Many of the things which have survived from Roman times have been covered by soil and need digging up. This is what **archaeologists** do. They dig in the ground and find remains from the past. Of course archaeologists don't just dig at random. They usually know where Roman remains can be found because they have had clues.

Archaeologists' clues

- Something Roman has been found nearby (like a piece of pottery or a brooch).
- A Roman writer says there was a camp or fort in a particular place.
- Places where there were once buildings can be spotted from the air.
- Local place names sometimes have Roman connections. For example chester or caster as name endings, as in Colchester (chester means fort).

Source B

Some of the things the Romans built were so huge that they have survived without breaking into tiny pieces. For example the Romans built a stadium called the Colosseum, which could hold 50,000 people. There's still plenty of it to look at!

A Roman inscription on stone found on Hadrian's Wall. It tells us that the Twentieth Legion built that part of the wall.

Source A

People like Tacitus, Suetonius, Cassius Dio and Livy have provided us with much valuable information. You will be reading some of their works as you go through this book.

Source D

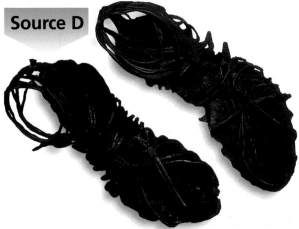

Archaeologists are particularly interested in finding everyday objects. They tell us useful things about ordinary life in Roman times.

Roman writing

We are lucky that some Romans could read and write, and we have found lots of their writings. Archaeologists have even found a quarry in Britain where a brave Roman soldier carved an insult about the Emperor on a wall. If he had been caught he would have been in big trouble!

The Romans liked writing about history and we have found some of their books.

Source C

The Roman writer Suetonius describes the strange behaviour of the Emperor Nero (who had, of course, been dead for a long time when this was written!).

As soon as night fell he would snatch a hat and go down to the taverns, or prowl the streets in search of mischief. One of his games was to attack men on their way home from dinner, stab them, and drop their bodies down sewers. He would also break into shops and then set up a miniature market at the Palace to sell off the stolen goods!

Sir Mortimer Wheeler

Sir Mortimer Wheeler was a famous British archaeologist. He was born in 1890 and became Keeper of the London Museum in 1926. He ran the archaeological digs at Verulamium (St Albans) and Maiden Castle (see page 53).

From 1944 to 1948 Mortimer Wheeler was in charge of archaeological work in India, which was still under British rule at the time. He is famous for finding out about the Indus Valley civilization there. He discovered two major cities from this early civilization. He returned to England in 1948 and became Professor of Roman Archaeology in London. He was knighted as Sir Mortimer Wheeler in 1952, and died in 1976.

Sir Mortimer Wheeler is famous for the many archaeologial digs that he organized. He is also famous for writing books and making television programmes that explained the work of archaeologists to people who were not historians.

Archaeology is not just a matter of digging things up and writing down what you see. It also involves a great deal of science to work out exactly what has been found. A famous poet once said about archaeology that:

Guessing is always much more fun than knowing.

What he meant was that part of the fun of archaeology is working out what something tells you about the past. Source A is an example of a very unusual find, but it still told us interesting things!

Source A

Archaeologists excavating a site in York in the late 1970s made a most unusual discovery. Amongst their finds was a piece of human **faeces** dating back to the tenth century. The faeces had not decomposed but had become **mineralised** and so had survived intact. Investigations of the piece of faeces (which was 19.5 x 5.5 x 2.5 cm and weighed 234g) showed that its owner had eaten a kind of bran and had two different kinds of intestinal worms. What a job for the archaeologist!

Lindow man

In 1984 workmen found a body in a peat bog at Lindow Moss near Manchester Airport. A small section of bone was tested using a process known as 'carbon dating'. This measures the amount of radioactivity in an object. Scientists discovered that the body had been in the peat bog since around 500 BC! The acid in the peat had preserved the body so that it looked like it had been buried much more recently.

The body was taken to London and a team of experts carried out tests on 'Lindow man', as the body was now officially called (though the men who first found him called him Pete Marsh!).

The scientists photographed and x-rayed the body. They even had a camera pushed into his mouth to see what his brain looked like! They were excited to find his stomach still intact because the experts on nutrition could then tell what he had eaten before his death.

What we find – and what we know!

1 Lindow man's fingernails were not rough or jagged – so we think he might have worked with textiles which would have smoothed his nails.

2 Scientists discovered hairs from a fox on his body – so we think he may have been wearing a fox fur.

3 In Lindow man's stomach scientists found charred wheat and bran grains – so we know that his last meal included a kind of bread which had been burned during cooking!

4 A powerful microscope also found parasite eggs in the stomach – so we know that Lindow man had worms.

Tollund man

Tollund man died 400 years after Lindlow man. He was found in a peat bog in Denmark. He was strangled, probably a sacrifice, like Lindlow man.

There was a moment of hushed silence in the laboratory when a rope was found around the body's neck. Scientists called in experts to explain how the rope was tied. The experts told the scientists that the rope was a type of garrotte, used to strangle Lindow man! A closer look revealed that the body had other wounds too.

Source C

An extract from *The Sunday Times* magazine, 6th April 1997:

We know from the Roman historian Pliny that mistletoe played an important part in ancient ceremonies. Lindow man was found to have mistletoe in his stomach. Historians think that he drank mistletoe pollen because he was a sacrifice.

Lindow man is now on display at the British Museum in London.

Source D

Ian West, a forensic scientist from Guy's Hospital in London, explaining how he thinks Lindow man died:

X-rays show a wound on top of the head. A small piece of skull has been driven right into the head. This confirms that a narrow striking object, probably like a small axe, was used. And from the look of the wound it was used twice.

Under the chin the garrotte has cut into his skin and there is also a deep wound on the right hand side of the neck about two inches long. It looks like a cutting wound.

He has been hit on the head, rendered unconscious so he was unable to fight back, a garrotte has been tied around his neck, a stick put in the back and twisted, breaking his neck. The garrotte has cut into his neck and then he has been bled by a cut-throat wound over the jugular vein.

Source E

Dr Ian Stead, Deputy-Keeper at the British Museum, explains why he thinks Lindow man was killed:

Apart from the way he died, another factor which points towards his death having been connected with some sort of ceremony is the fact that he was naked. As far as we know the climate around Manchester at that time was even worse than it is today. So he would hardly have been wandering around naked!

1.3 CAN YOU ALWAYS TRUST HISTORICAL SOURCES?

Finding out about events in the past can be very annoying! One of the problems with studying history is that even when you have a lot of evidence you still can't be sure that you know what happened. The reason for this is that sometimes historians are not sure whether they can believe what they are being told (or as historians say, whether the evidence is 'reliable').

A historical source can be unreliable for a number of reasons. For example, the person providing the evidence might not be in a position to know exactly what happened. If you could go back in time and ask a British chief why the Romans invaded in AD 43, he would probably give you a list of reasons.

But because he was not in Rome when Claudius made his decision to invade, he would not really know. So his list of reasons would not be reliable.

However, the main reason why sources are sometimes unreliable is that people writing about events are often swayed by their own feelings. On page 5, Suetonius said some very nasty things about the Emperor Nero. Suetonius did not like Nero, so his account would not be reliable. It would be biased, or slanted, against Nero. Suetonius might not be telling lies, just seeing things in a critical way because he did not like the Emperor.

Now let's have a look at some biased sources in action:

SUPER NEWCHESTER SEE OFF MANHAMPTON

Newchester gave a wonderful display of attacking football on Saturday. From start to finish they launched a series of skilful attacks on the Manhampton goal and could easily have been several goals in the lead by half-time.

In the second half their non-stop pressure finally paid off when they were awarded two penalties. Dave Smith calmly beat the despairing Manhampton goalkeeper to score both penalties. Manhampton were so rattled by the speed and strength of the Newchester forwards that they finally conceded a third goal late in the second half.

Newchester scorers: Smith penalty 65 mins, Smith penalty 70 mins, Jones (own goal 90 mins).

Manhampton scorers: Brown 15 minutes, Green 30 minutes.

Biased sources

It seems odd to have a made up modern football match in a history book. But it is important to realize that all sources can be biased. Sometimes the bias is obvious. Sometimes not.

Almost everyone who gives you information could be doing so in a biased way – newspapers, the TV and the radio, as well as people in the past. It is not just advertisers who are trying to get you to think what they want you to think.

So remember

What you have been looking at on these pages are examples of reports which are exaggerated. This has been done to help show you how reports can be biased. It is unlikely that even the most biased newspaper will be one-sided in its reporting. Remember, though, that you are going to read about the Romans and most of the written sources are by Romans themselves. These authors might be completely reliable and might be telling us the exact truth. Then again, when they tell us that the Romans are great, they might just be exaggerating a little bit, so take care.

BRAVE MANHAMPTON JUST FAIL TO HOLD ON
NEWCHESTER 3 MANHAMPTON 2

Manhampton must consider themselves one of the unluckiest sides in the history of football after Saturday's narrow defeat at Newchester. By half-time Manhampton had already scored two great goals from Brown and Green and looked likely to win easily.

In the second half two more goals were scored, but they were disallowed even though no-one could see what was wrong with them. Then as the game came near to its end the Newchester centre forward tripped over the Manhampton goalkeeper and the referee mysteriously gave a penalty. The goalkeeper was carried off and Green had to go in goal (the first time he had ever played there). He almost saved the penalty, but it squeezed in under his body. Five minutes later an even more bizarre penalty was awarded and Green almost saved that too.

It looked like unlucky Manhampton would have to settle for a draw until in the last few seconds a shot from a Newchester forward hit the referee, deflected into the face of Jones and into his own goal.

Imagine if in the year AD 3000 students were given the topic 'Life in the 1990s' to write a project on.

Unfortunately for them a disaster in the year AD 2500 wiped out almost all the historical sources from the 1990s.

Only two sources survived.

Source A

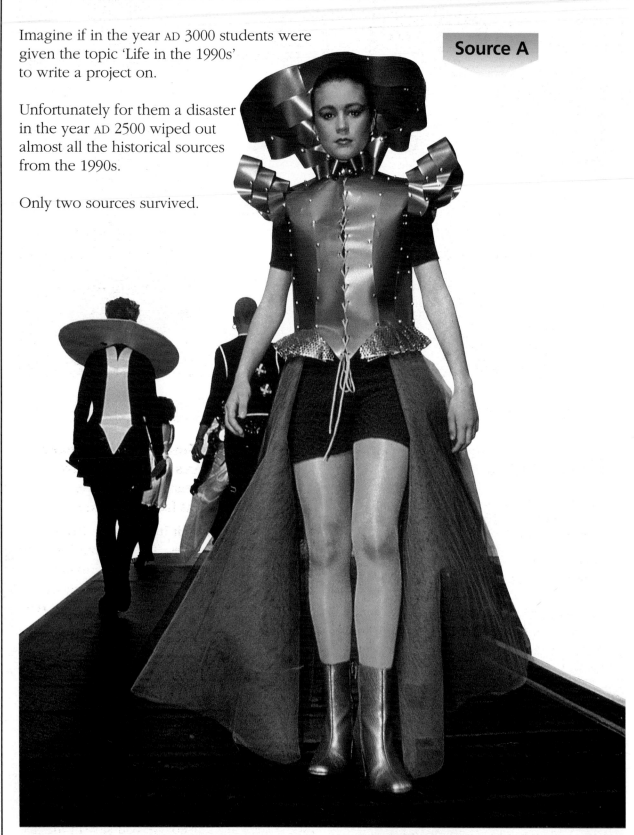

A photograph from the 1990s.

A photograph from the 1990s.

Thucydides

Thucydides was a Greek writer who lived in the fifth century BC (the 400s). He is thought by many people to be 'the first historian'. Why?

Before Thucydides wrote his *History of the Peloponnesian War*, people who wrote about the past had seen their job as story telling. They were not very concerned about getting their facts right. They were not very concerned about being unbiased, either. They tried to fill the past with exciting events and skipped the parts where nothing happened. If the Greeks were telling a story they would make the Greek warriors brave and their opponents cowards.

Thucydides did not do this. He tried very hard to tell exactly what happened and when it happened. He was more concerned with getting the history right than with telling an exciting story. Some people at the time said they found his book dull. But is is very useful to modern historians.

Learning about history – a summary

The first eight pages in this book have helped you understand some of the problems historians face. These are:

1 Historians get their information from many different places. The information they have might come from books, remains found in the ground, old manuscripts or even by talking to people who witnessed a particular event.

2 It is very rare for historians to have enough information to get a complete picture. As there are often gaps in their information, historians sometimes have to make guesses about what has happened. This is why there are times when historians write different accounts, or interpretations, about the same event.

3 Historians also have to check sources to see if they are biased. As you saw in the last unit people sometimes allow their opinions to influence how they see things.

How did Rome begin?

Historians do not really know how and when Rome first became a city. It is difficult to find out because there are no writings from the time. We could look at what is left of the early city in the ground. But there is very little of this to see, as the site has been built over many times.

The archaeological evidence we have found tells us that about 700 years before Christ was born a small **settlement** of farmers lived in mud huts near the river Tiber in an area of Italy called 'Latium'. The farmers had built their settlement on a hill, which later became known as the Palatine Hill. There were seven hills near the river and soon each had a settlement built on it. In time the settlements grew and eventually joined up to make one city. This was Rome – the city that would one day rule the world.

The Roman version of the story

When Rome became famous, the Romans thought it did not sound important enough that the city had started when a few small farms joined together. They wanted a much more dramatic story. They liked the stories that had been passed down between people about how Rome had started. The most famous of these stories was that of Romulus and Remus. This story was first written down in 200 BC. It became so popular that the legend of Romulus and Remus was taught to all Roman schoolchildren. Soon it was the official explanation of how the city started.

Map of Italy showing Latium in around 700 BC.

Tarquinius

Tarquinius was the last king of Rome. He lived from about 534 to 510 BC. We know that he increased the power of Rome – it is said that during his reign Rome took control of all of Latium. He is also said to have been the king who began building towns around a forum.

However, he seems to have tried to increase his own power, along with that of Rome. This made him very unpopular. He was thrown out of Rome in 509 BC and rule by kings was replaced by the Roman Republic.

Source A

A statue of the she-wolf feeding the twins Romulus and Remus. The she-wolf was carved in the 6th century BC, but the twins were not added until much later.

THE LEGEND OF ROMULUS AND REMUS

The city of Alba Longa, on the banks of the river Tiber, was ruled by King Numitor. He was overthrown by his wicked brother, Amulius. King Numitor had a daughter, Rhea Silvia, who married Mars, the God of War, and then gave birth to twin brothers Romulus and Remus. When Amulius heard, he ordered that the boys should be drowned in the river. But the servant ordered to murder them took pity on them and left them floating in a cradle on the river.

The cradle washed up on the banks of the river and the boys were found by a she-wolf. She let them feed on her milk. Then a shepherd found the boys, took them home and brought them up as his own children. When they grew up they found out what Amulius had done. They led an attack on Alba Longa in which Amulius was killed and Numitor was made King once more.

Romulus and Remus decided to build their own city, but argued about which of the seven hills they should build it on. They agreed that the gods would decide. They would stare at the sky and whoever saw a vulture could choose. Remus was the first to see a vulture, but Romulus said he had won because he saw twelve.

Romulus began to build a city on the Palatine hill. He built a wall to protect the city. Remus felt cheated and jumped over the wall to show Romulus that he thought his new city was useless. Romulus was so cross that he killed Remus and shouted: *So perish all who ever cross my walls.*

Romulus completed his city on 21 April 753 BC and it was named Rome in his honour. Some years later, after making laws about how his city should be ruled, Romulus disappeared. This is supposed to have happened in the middle of a thunderstorm in front of all the people of Rome. Romulus was now said to be a god and was worshipped under the name Quirinus.

Historians don't believe the Romulus and Remus legend, but they do think that the city of Rome was founded about 800 years before the birth of Christ. This is actually very close to 753 BC, the date given in the Romulus and Remus legend. What there is no doubt about is that Rome eventually grew to be the world's most important city. This happened in a number of stages.

Stage 1: Rome controls Italy

Until 509 BC Rome was ruled by seven kings. The last of these kings was Tarquinius Superbus whose name means 'proud'. Roman writers tell us that Tarquinius was so proud that he was driven out of the city and the people decided not to have a king any more. Instead Rome would be a **Republic** which meant that the people of Rome would choose their leaders.

At about this time the Romans began to take over many neighbouring tribes and cities. In 390 BC Rome was attacked and almost destroyed by invading Gauls (from what we now call France). However the Romans recovered and by about 250 BC they had taken control of almost the whole of Italy. When the Romans defeated their opponents, they did not take over their land. Instead they allowed the people they had conquered to keep their lands in return for becoming Rome's ally and accepting that the Romans were their masters.

Roman possessions and provinces

Rome controlled most of Italy by 265 BC.

HORATIUS THE HERO

A legend often told by the Romans is that of Horatius Cocles (Horatio the one-eyed) and his brave stand against the Etruscans:

Rome was being attacked by the Etruscans. Only a bridge stood between Rome and the enemy. Horatius Cocles, a Roman soldier, bravely volunteered to stand on the enemy-held side of the river and fight off the Etruscans. He fought them single-handed until their attack became too much for him. Horatius jumped into the river and swam back to the Roman side. The jubilant Etruscans ran onto the bridge, only to find that the Romans were already chopping it down. Before the Etruscans could get to the other side, the bridge collapsed with them on it. Horatius the Hero was rewarded with as much land as he could plough in a day.

Stage 2: Rome versus Carthage

As Rome grew, it began to come into more contact with foreign countries. Roman **merchants** began to sell more goods in countries with a coastline on the Mediterranean Sea and made a great deal of money. This soon upset another city which had been used to controlling trade in this area – Carthage. It wasn't long before Rome and Carthage were at war.

Carthage was very powerful, with a large empire in north Africa and southern Spain. The Romans fought three wars with Carthage. In the first Carthaginian war (264–241 BC) the Romans built their first navy and captured the island of Sicily.

This was their first **province** – land captured outside their own country.

Later they also took Sardinia and Corsica from Carthage. The second Carthaginian war (218–201 BC) very nearly saw Rome destroyed. The great Carthaginian general, Hannibal, brought his army into Italy. But Hannibal was defeated. Rome won the war. Carthage could no longer match the power of Rome. To make sure that there would be no further problems, Rome fought a third war (149–146 BC). Carthage was burned to the ground and the land on which the city had stood was ploughed over. The people of Carthage were sold into slavery.

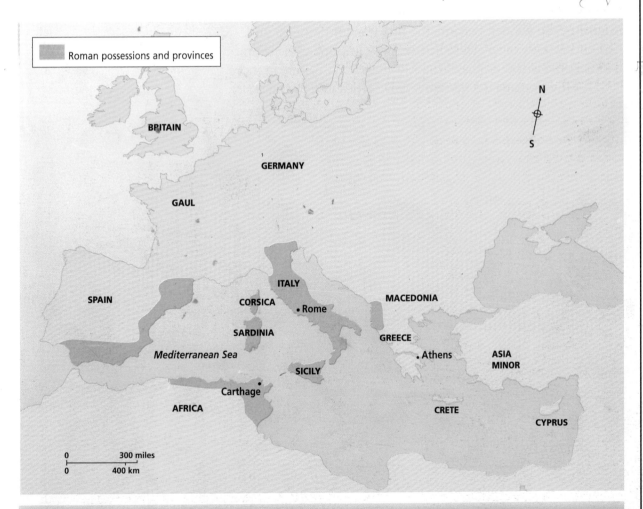

The beginnings of an empire: lands controlled by Rome after the second defeat of Carthage, 201 BC.

Stage 3: Into the eastern Mediterranean

The victory over the Carthaginians had brought Rome new land to control. Soon they had extended this land to include most of Spain and southern Gaul (modern-day France).

At the same time the Romans took over more land in the east. By 121 BC they had taken over Greece, Macedonia and Asia Minor (modern-day Turkey). As each new area was conquered it became a Roman province, part of the Roman Empire with a governor appointed by Rome. The governor made sure that the province was ruled the way the Romans wanted. The people of the provinces paid taxes to Rome which helped make the city very rich.

Stage 4: The Empire at its largest

The Roman Empire continued to get bigger over the next few centuries. In the 1st century BC Julius Caesar captured the parts of Spain and Gaul which were not already Roman provinces. In 27 BC, after a war between various Roman leaders, Augustus, the winner, became the first Roman Emperor and had enormous power. This showed how important the Empire had become to the Romans. Later Roman Emperors won more land for the Romans in Germany, Asia, Africa and in Britain.

Source A

The Roman writer, Livy, writing in the 1st century BC, talked about how Rome thought it should rule the world.

The gods want the city of Rome to be the capital of all the countries of the world. They shall practise warfare so that no humans shall be able to resist the armies of Rome.

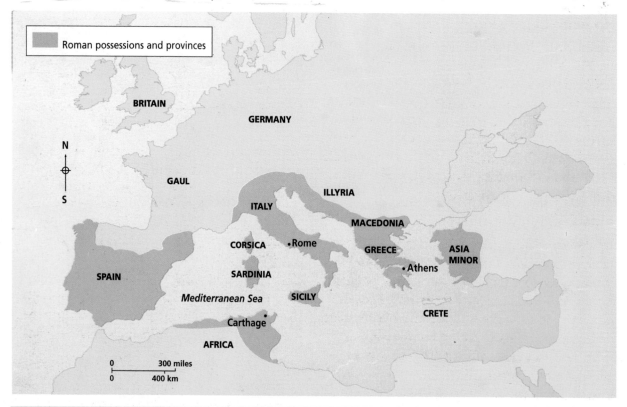

Roman expansion in western Europe and the eastern Mediterranean up to 121 BC.

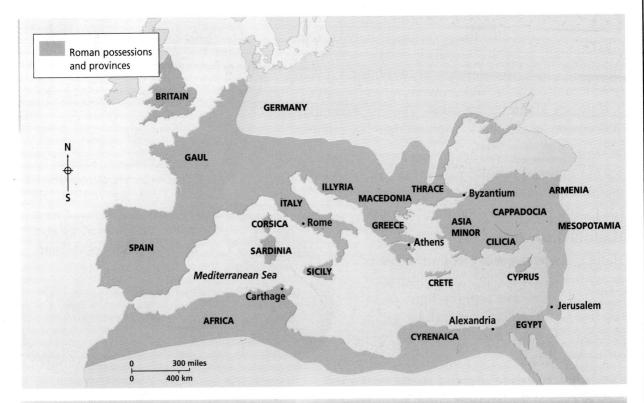

The Empire at its largest: the Roman Empire in about AD 120.

No more expansion

By the time that Hadrian became Emperor in AD 117 Rome had a huge Empire. Hadrian decided that it was big enough, and during his reign no new lands were conquered. Indeed, it was Hadrian who built the famous wall across the top of Britain to mark the boundary of the Empire. If you lived north of Newcastle the Romans thought you were a barbarian and didn't want you in their Empire.

A divided empire

By the time of Hadrian's death in AD 128 the Roman Empire had reached its maximum size. It was now so large that capturing new lands would simply make it too difficult to govern properly. In time the Romans discovered that defending and governing what they already captured was very difficult. This is why in AD 285 the Emperor Diocletian split the Empire in two. From then onwards, there were usually at least two Emperors, very often one in the east and one in the west.

Hadrian

Hadrian's parents were Spanish, but he was born in Rome in AD 76. His father died in AD 85. Hadrian was adopted by a relative, Trajan, who became emperor of Rome in AD 98.

Hadrian worked hard for the Empire. He fought in several wars. From AD 102 onwards, he was governor of several provinces of the Roman Empire. Trajan expanded the Empire rapidly, more interested in conquering lands than in making sure that Rome could sensibly hold and govern them. In AD 117 Trajan died. Hadrian replaced him as emperor.

Hadrian was the first emperor to consider that the Empire was big enough. He stopped expanding the Empire. He gave back some of the land that Trajan had seized. He decided to build a series of frontier fortifications all around the edges of the Empire. One of the most famous of these was built in northern Britain. Hadrian's Wall is still there.

One of the most exciting stories in the Roman period concerns the invasion of Italy by the Carthaginian general, Hannibal, in 217 BC. This was such a dramatic event that over two hundred years later Roman schoolchildren were writing essays and poetry about the invasion. The cry 'Hannibal is at the gates' was used to frighten naughty children.

We know a great deal about this story because it was set out in detail by a Roman writer called Livy. We will use his account to find out exactly what happened (his words will be in *italics*).

Hannibal the boy

Hannibal was the son of a Carthaginian general, Hamilcar Barca. Hamilcar was defeated at the hands of the Romans in the first Carthaginian war and wanted revenge. He made sure that his son felt the same way too:

Hannibal as a nine year old, asked his father to take him to see the army in Spain. His father took him to an altar and made him swear an oath saying that he would prove himself, as soon as he could, to be an enemy of the Roman people.

Hannibal the general

As Hannibal grew up he proved to be a skilled general and at the age of 29 became commander of the Carthaginian forces:

He was fearless in carrying out dangerous tasks. Hard work could not tire his body, nor dampen his spirit. He could endure both heat and cold. He did not use a soft bed and was often seen wrapped only in a blanket sleeping along with the soldiers.

War!

In 218 BC Hannibal captured the town of Saguntum in Spain. According to the peace treaty after the first Carthaginian war this town was under Roman control. So the Romans declared war. They expected to fight the war in Spain or in Africa. Hannibal could not invade Italy from the sea because the Romans controlled it and would sink his ships. They never dreamt that he would lead his forces across 1,500 miles and through two mountain ranges into Italy.

Source A

A statue of Hannibal, probably from the time of his invasion of Italy. It was found in the town of Capua, which was one of the Italian cities which supported Hannibal during the war.

LIVY

Titus Livius was a Roman noble who lived from 59 BC to AD 17. He wrote a history of Rome from 735 BC to 9 BC and his books were widely used in Roman schools. Some modern historians say that his work is not always accurate because he slanted his stories in favour of the Romans.

When Hannibal set out from Carthago Nova in the spring of 218 BC he had an army of around 100,000 men made up of a variety of people, from Africa, Spain and Gaul. He also had 37 elephants, which the Carthaginians used in battle to break up enemy ranks. As he marched north towards Italy he had to fight off attacks from hostile tribes. He also had to cross several large rivers, such as the Ebro and the Rhone.

After crossing the river Rhone, Hannibal began his march across the Alps. It was a march which frightened many of his men:

Hannibal asked: Why are you afraid? On the other side of those mountains is Italy. No part of the earth reaches the sky. The ancient Gauls crossed the Alps with their wives and children. You are soldiers carrying nothing but your weapons. So either admit that the Gauls are better men than you or else follow me and look forward to the end of your journey at the gates of Rome.

It also astonished the Romans. They had sent a force by sea led by Scipio to cut off Hannibal's army as it left Spain. Scipio arrived at the foot of the Alps to find Hannibal gone. He immediately put his men back in ships and returned to Italy.

How did the elephants cross the Rhone?

The Carthaginians built a raft fifty feet wide and two hundred feet long. They secured this to the river bank. To this they attached another raft of the same size and covered the whole thing in earth so that it looked like firm earth. The elephants were taken across the first raft and onto the second. They thought they were on firm ground. Then the second raft was set free and the elephants were afloat. After several journeys all the elephants were across.

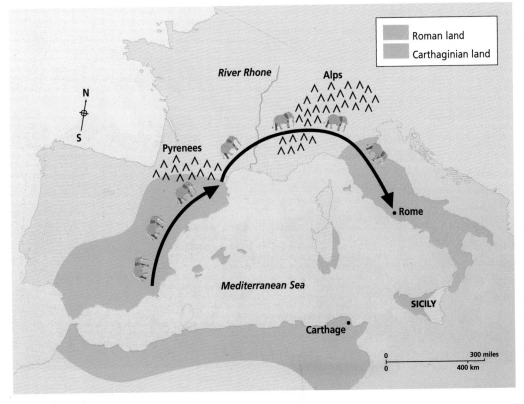

Roman land

Carthaginian land

River Rhone

Alps

Pyrenees

N

S

Rome

Mediterranean Sea

SICILY

Carthage

0 300 miles

0 400 km

The route Hannibal took to Rome

Journey through the Alps

Hannibal's journey was difficult and dangerous. Even today we do not know exactly which route he took through the Alps, but we know it wasn't an easy one. From time to time his army was ambushed by hostile local tribes. Eventually his army reached the top of the mountains and Hannibal promised his men that: *The rest of your journey will be smooth and downhill.* It was downhill, but it was definitely not smooth! The descent into Italy was even steeper than the ascent from Gaul and many men died on the slippery rocks:

Men who made the smallest stumble could not stop themselves from falling. When they fell they rolled down on top of other men causing them to fall. In this way men and animals fell to their deaths.

A difficult obstacle

Then they came to a dead end. A huge boulder, bigger than a house, had fallen across the path and could not be moved. Nor could any way be found over or around it. As Livy says, the Carthaginians seemed: *to have reached the end of their journey.* But Hannibal had other ideas. He set his men to work destroying the boulder.

How the boulder was destroyed

Hannibal ordered his men to build a huge fire under the rock. When it was hot he told them to pour vinegar on it and to attack it with picks and hammers. The acid in the vinegar helped split the rock and eventually, after four days' work, it shattered into moveable pieces.

The descent into Italy continued and fifteen days after they had arrived at the Alps the Carthaginians were through them. 60,000 men had set off into the Alps, only 23,000 made it to the other side.

A modern painting of Hannibal crossing the Alps in 218 BC.

Source B

Hannibal reaches Italy

Hannibal's army was now in Italy and was soon to meet the Romans. The Roman army sent with Scipio to meet Hannibal in Gaul finally caught up with him at the river Trebia – and was soon destroyed by Hannibal's forces. After resting over the winter Hannibal's forces moved on and crushed another Roman army at Lake Trasimene, where they killed 15,000 Romans.

There was terrible panic in Rome, where Hannibal was expected any day. But Hannibal did not have enough men or equipment to capture the city. The man in charge of the Roman forces, Quintus Fabius, knew this. He decided to avoid a battle and wear Hannibal down. This seemed to work, but many Romans thought it was cowardly. They could not believe that their armies were letting Hannibal plunder Italy. Fabius was replaced and two new generals, Paullus and Varro, led an army of 90,000 men against Hannibal. The battle was one of Rome's greatest disasters and 70,000 of their troops were killed. Hannibal lost only 6000 men. Fabius had obviously been right.

On the morning after the battle at Cannae the scene was shocking. Thousands of Romans were dying on the battlefield. Some begged people to cut their throats and put them out of their misery. Others were found with their heads plunged into the earth. They had dug holes and suffocated themselves by throwing earth over their faces. One Carthaginian with lacerated ears and nose was found under a dead Roman. The Roman had been wounded and so could not use his hands. As he died he had torn at his enemy with his bare teeth.

Hannibal is defeated

Despite his victory, Hannibal still did not feel ready to march on Rome and was never able to capture the city. In 210 BC Scipio 'the Younger' (the son of the general defeated at the river Trebia) took an army to Spain and began winning battles. When Scipio crossed to Carthage, the Carthaginian commanders called Hannibal back to save the city. But at the Battle of Zama (202 BC) Hannibal was defeated and the Carthaginians lost the war.

Hannibal later fled to Asia, and in the year 182 BC he took poison to avoid being captured by the enemy he had so nearly destroyed.

Quintus Fabius

Quintus Fabius was the Roman commander who held off Hannibal during the Second Carthaginian War. He was called 'Cunctator', which means 'the Delayer', after this.

Fabius was elected dictator in AD 217. Neither he nor his policies were popular with everyone. Many Romans felt that avoiding battle was not the way to treat an enemy. They thought Fabius should send the army in to fight Hannibal. They were sure the Roman army would win.

Fabius's policy was proved right. When he was replaced by Paullus and Varro, they marched into battle against Hannibal at Cannae – to be badly beaten. Fabius died in AD 203.

By the 1st century AD the Romans were in control of a huge Empire and few people dared challenge their rule. The reason for this was quite simple. The Roman army was so powerful that any opposition was quickly dealt with. It took great courage to challenge the Roman army and almost always ended in defeat.

How was the Roman army organised?

Legions and centuries

The main part of the Roman army was the **legion**. This was made up of about 5000 men under the command of the **legate**.

The legion was divided into about ten cohorts, each of which was made up of six **centuries**. The centuries were commanded by a centurion. The century once had a hundred men it, which is how it got its name. However, later there were only about 60–80 men in each century.

Centurions

The centurions were very important men in the Roman legions. They were responsible for training the soldiers under their command and for making sure everyone obeyed orders. Some centurions were noted for their cruel treatment of the legionaries.

Standards

Each century had its own its own emblem or **standard**. This was carried by the century's standard bearer, a very experienced and trusted soldier. All the legions also had an imperial standard, which was an eagle. This was carried by the legionary standard bearer. For a legion to lose its eagle in battle was a great disgrace.

Source A

Tacitus, writing in the 1st century AD.

One centurion called Lucilius was killed by his own troops in a mutiny. They hated him because of the punishments he handed out to his men. He was nick-named 'give me another' because that's what he said every time he broke his vine-stick on a soldier's back.

How to make a Roman legion

Step 1 Take eight men and form them into a group called a **tent**.

Step 2 Combine ten tents together into a **century** of 80 men under the command of a **centurion**.

Step 3 Put six centuries together to make a **cohort** of 480 men.

CENTURY	CENTURY	CENTURY
1	2	3
CENTURY	CENTURY	CENTURY
4	5	6

Step 4 Put ten cohorts together to make 4800 men. Add about 500 clerks and skilled tradesmen and you have a **legion**.

How the Roman army was organised.

Javelin: Just over two metres long. Made out of wood with a metal tip which bent when pulled out of an enemy's shield.

Helmet: Made of iron to protect the head, face and neck without blocking hearing or vision.

Sword: About 50 cm long and 5 cm wide. It usually had a handle of wood and was worn in a **scabbard**. A double-bladed dagger would sometimes be worn opposite the sword, on the left.

Metal jacket: Metal strips held together by leather straps. It was so heavy soldiers had to help each other put it on.

Belt: The sword and dagger were attached to the belt and strips of leather covered with metal discs hung from it.

Tunic: Made of coarse wool; thigh-length. In the later years of the Empire breeches (short trousers) were sometimes worn.

Shield: This was made of wood with a strengthening metal stud in the centre. It was 1.6 m tall.

Equipment: Soldiers had to carry all their tools, weapons and cooking equipment with them when they marched. They also carried blankets and bedding.

Sandals: Made from leather and laced up with leather thongs. Iron hobnails were hammered into the sole to enable the sandal to stand to the miles of marching.

Becoming a legionary

To become a legionary was not always easy. You did not have to be a Roman to join a legion, but you had to prove that you were a Roman citizen. (From 90 BC all Italians were Roman citizens and many people in other countries in the Roman Empire were made Roman citizens as a reward. See page 16.) You also had to be physically fit and at least 1.6 m tall. Once a man was accepted into the legion he swore an oath of loyalty and began his training. Being a Roman legionary was not a short-term job. Men were expected to stay in the army for 25 years.

Training

Most legionaries joined the army between the ages of eighteen and twenty, although there was a soldier in a legion in Britain who was just fourteen. Such young soldiers were very rare. Training was very tough, and it was important that the legionaries were very fit. They had to carry out three 30 km marches each month. On each march the legionary would carry more than 25 kilos of equipment.

Legionaries would also learn **drill**, or marching. This was very important for carrying out **manoeuvres** in battle. Training to use weapons was also important. New recruits were given a shield and sword twice the weight of the real weapons and learned how to use them with skill and speed. Legionaries also learned how to throw the javelin, an essential part of their fighting equipment.

Who else was in the army?

As well as the legionaries, the Roman army also contained a large number of **auxiliaries**. These were groups of soldiers from lands conquered by the Romans who volunteered to fight in the Roman army.

Source C

The Jewish writer, Josephus, describing Roman training in the 1st century AD. He ought to know what he was talking about as he fought in battles against the Romans!

The Romans do not sit around waiting for war to break out and then start training men to fight. It looks as if they are born with weapons in their hands. They never stop training and every soldier puts all he has into training, just as if he was in a real war. Their enemies are never a match for the Romans, and the Romans always win.

Many of these auxiliary soldiers had special skills. For example, the Romans were not particularly good horsemen, so the cavalry was made up mainly of men from areas where fighting on horseback was common, such as Gaul.

Other auxiliaries were skilled archers, or lethal with a stone sling. But the majority of auxiliaries fought with a sword and a short spear. Some of them wore no armour, though many had a type of **chain-mail** for protection.

The Romans thought the auxiliaries were second-class soldiers and they were paid only about a third of a legionary's wages. Auxiliaries were not Roman citizens, and they also did not have the rigorous training of the legionary. They were excellent for patrols, frontier duties and raids, but the serious fighting was usually the job of the legions.

Auxiliaries usually served for 25 years and then became Roman citizens. But the real bonus was that their children became Roman citizens as well. That meant that their sons could apply to become legionaries.

Source D

The tombstone of Marcus Favonius Facilis.

MARCUS FAVONIUS FACILIS

In 1868 archaeologists digging in Colchester, Essex, discovered the tombstone of Marcus Favonius Facilis, a centurion in the Twentieth Legion.

His tombstone had been put up by two of his slaves, Verecundus and Novicius whom Facilis had freed in his will. The stone provides us with an excellent example of how a centurion looked in the 1st century AD. Facilis has the centurion's stick in his right hand and a sword in his left hand. We get an idea of Roman fashions because although Facilis is in standard uniform, his hair is in the same style as that seen on statues of the Emperor Claudius from the same time.

The tombstone had been knocked down and broken into two pieces. Archaeologists think that this happened when Boudica's rebels attacked Colchester in AD 60 (see page 54).

Gaius Marius

Gaius Marius is seen as the person who made the Roman army into a professional fighting force. He was born in about 155 BC and became a Roman politician. In 107 BC he was elected as consul. He managed to get re-elected several times, even though a consul was supposed not to have the job for any longer than two years.

While he was consul, he had the power to change the army. He made it possible for citizens who did not own land to join the army and make the army their career.

Marius was driven out of Rome in 88 BC, but returned in 87 BC with a large army. He took over the city, killed his opponents and became consul again. He died in 86 BC, just after he had been elected consul for the seventh time.

On the battlefield

The Romans were highly skilled in battle. Their weapons and tactics were not really any better than their enemies', but they were highly disciplined. A Roman soldier would never break ranks and run from the battlefield. Before a battle the Romans would line up their forces with the legion in the centre and cavalry and auxiliaries on either side. The soldiers marched forward until they were within twenty metres of the enemy and then threw their javelins. Then, before the enemy had a chance to recover, they charged with their swords. Using their swords and shields they would try to knock a hole in the enemy's formation and work their way outwards from there. Sometimes archers or **slingers** were used to cause chaos in the enemy ranks before an advance.

Attacking a fortified area

The Romans were excellent at fighting on the battlefield, but they spent much more of their time attacking enemy bases which had been **fortified**, or made stronger with walls and ditches. The Romans had very effective methods and weapons for attacking these sorts of fortifications.

Catapults

Small catapults fired a wooden arrow with a deadly metal head. Larger catapults fired stones which ranged from the size of a tennis ball to over 45 kilos in weight. These catapults had a range of almost half a mile. One writer tells us that a soldier's head was once knocked off and carried over 500 m by a stone from a catapult.

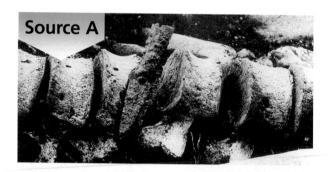

Source A

The victim of a Roman catapult. This skeleton was found at Maiden Castle in Britain. The bolt head is still lodged in the spine of the unfortunate Briton.

Battering rams

Battering rams were used to weaken walls. Most rams were made from tree trunks, strengthened with a metal head and suspended from ropes inside a shed big enough to hold up to thirty men. The shed was there to protect the soldiers as they attacked the walls.

Testudos

Sometimes the Romans linked shields over their heads to form a *testudo* (tortoise). This protected them from attack from above. Some writers say that soldiers were trained to form strong *testudos* by having chariots driven over them.

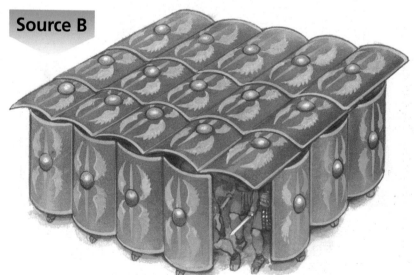

Source B

A group of soldiers in a *testudo* formation.

Siege towers

These were tall towers pushed right up against the walls of a fortification. On the top soldiers would throw their javelins and try to climb over the walls; below other soldiers would use battering rams to attack the walls.

Roman soldiers attack a fortress from inside a siege tower. Note the arrows being shot from the top, and the battering ram at the bottom of the tower.

Source C

Of course Roman legionaries spent much more time at peace than at war. Roman legions were sent all over the Empire to stop trouble, not to start it. Some parts of the Empire had hundreds of years of peace under Roman rule. But, the fact that there was no fighting did not mean that the Roman legionary had nothing to do.

Army work

Every time a legion moved a new camp had to be built. They dug trenches 1.5 m deep and 2.4 m wide all round the new camp. Then some unlucky soldiers were picked for sentry duty. It was their job to act as guards through the night. This task was so important that any legionary found asleep at his post would be beaten to death by his fellow soldiers with large sticks.

Even when a legion was settled in an area there was plenty of work to do. If the area had just been conquered fortifications had to be built – or even a new fort. Apart from the long hours of training there were always routine jobs to be done (see Source A).

Building work

Sometimes soldiers had to help with major building projects, like building the roads for which the Romans became so famous. It was the Roman army which built Hadrian's Wall, stretching from coast to coast across northern England.

Free time

Of course soldiers did get some time off. Soldiers based in Italy might have been given leave to visit their families. Those based in a foreign country were much less likely to get leave.

Source A

A list of jobs for Roman legionaries. This is part of a list found in Egypt from the reign of the Emperor Domitian (AD 81–86).

Gaius Domitius Celer:
Resting

Gaius Julius Valens:
Digging ditches

Marcus Arrius Niger:
Cleaning barracks

Publius Clodius Secundus:
Cleaning boots

Gaius Aemilius Valens:
Working in the armoury (where weapons were kept and repaired)

Roman soldiers building a fort. This is one of the scenes carved on a column built during the reign of Emperor Trajan (AD 98–117) to tell the story of his military campaigns.

Source B

So most soldiers had to fill their own leisure time inside the camp. Although gambling was supposed to be forbidden, the Romans played a variety of games where money was staked on the throw of a dice or even on a form of noughts and crosses. The Romans were very keen on board games as well.

Source C

Extract from a letter to a Roman soldier found at the Roman fort of Vindolanda in Northumberland.

I have sent you pairs of socks from Sattua, two pairs of sandals and two pairs of underpants. Greetings to all your messmates. I pray that you live in the greatest good fortune.

Source D

An article in *The Times* newspaper on 26 September 1996.

Trajan

Trajan was born in Spain in AD 52. He became a soldier in the Roman army. He worked his way up through the Roman government. He was made consul in AD 91. The Emperor Domitian trusted him enough to make him governor of the province of Germania in AD 96.

Trajan became emperor in AD 98. He introduced a system to help the poor. He had a new forum and baths built in the city. His armies won many victories. Trajan's column (Source B) celebrates one in AD 106. He died in AD 117.

ROMAN BOARD GAME FOUND AT BURIAL SITE

A mysterious board game that kept the Romans amused down the centuries has been found laid out and ready to play in a 2000–year–old burial site in Essex.

The game was buried alongside the bones of its owner, apparently to provide entertainment in the afterlife.

The archaeologist who found it said 'It is the first time that a game like this has been found virtually intact, and with all the pieces in place, just as they would have been in around the year AD 50. What makes it so special is that we have found the outline of the board as well. The original wood had crumbled to dust, but the edges were made of metal and are still there. First we uncovered the whole row of the blue pieces and we said "Wouldn't it be great if the white pieces were there as well?" – and then like magic, they appeared.'

Glass beads

Hinge

55 cm

Wooden board

40 cm

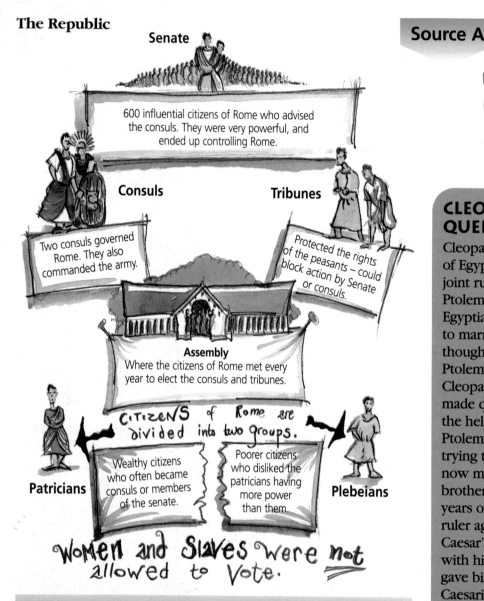

The Republic

Senate

600 influential citizens of Rome who advised the consuls. They were very powerful, and ended up controlling Rome.

Consuls

Two consuls governed Rome. They also commanded the army.

Tribunes

Protected the rights of the peasants – could block action by Senate or consuls.

Assembly
Where the citizens of Rome met every year to elect the consuls and tribunes.

CITIZENS of Rome are divided into two groups.

Patricians

Wealthy citizens who often became consuls or members of the senate.

Poorer citizens who disliked the patricians having more power than them.

Plebeians

WOMEN and SLAVES were not allowed to vote.

Rome was ruled by kings until 509 BC. After that Rome was a Republic – a state without a king or president. This is how the Republic worked.

The Republic breaks down

Until about 100 BC the consuls only called up men to fight in the army when they needed them. After 100 BC Rome had a professional army of full-time soldiers. Some people were worried, quite rightly, that the army might decide to take over the city. In 87 BC General Gaius Marius did just that. He killed anyone against whom he had the slightest grudge. Just a few years later another general, Lucius Sulla, captured the city and made himself dictator. But perhaps the most famous of all the generals who seized power in Rome was Julius Caesar.

Source A

CLEOPATRA – QUEEN OF EGYPT

Cleopatra became Queen of Egypt age 17. She was joint ruler with her brother Ptolemy XII. Because of Egyptian custom she had to marry Ptolemy – even though he was only 12. Ptolemy's advisors drove Cleopatra out. She was made queen again with the help of Julius Caesar. Ptolemy drowned in battle trying to stop this. Cleopatra now married her younger brother, Ptolemy XIII (11 years old!) and was joint ruler again. She became Caesar's mistress and lived with him in Rome. She gave birth to a son, Caesarion, who was said to be Caesar's child.

After Caesar's assassination she returned to Egypt, poisoned Ptolemy and made Caesarion her joint ruler. In 41 BC she met Mark Anthony who fell in love with her. Later they were married and had three children.

After the Battle of Actium, she and Anthony committed suicide. Octavian had Caesarion put to death and Rome took over Egypt.

Julius Caesar

Caesar came from a leading Roman family. He was a brave soldier and in 59 BC was elected consul. After his year in office he was put in charge of the Roman army in Gaul. After seven years Caesar defeated all the tribes of Gaul.

A Roman coin with Caesar's head on it. The inscription reads *Caesar Dict Perpetuo* meaning 'Caesar Dictator for life'.

Growing resentment

Caesar's success made him enemies in Rome. One of these was General Pompey. Soon Pompey and Caesar were involved in a civil war to see who would control Rome. Caesar won and was made 'Dictator for life'. His head began to appear on coins. This was an honour usually reserved for the gods or dead officials. Many of the Senators resented Caesar's power. On 15 March 44 BC some of the senators decided the time had come to get rid of Caesar.

Assassination!

The story of Caesar's death is told by the writer Suetonius:

It was about 10 o'clock when Caesar set off for the Senate. As he went someone handed him a note containing details of the plot against him, but he just added it to all his other papers which he intended to read later.

As Caesar sat down, a group of conspirators crowded around pretending to pay their respects. Cimber caught hold of his shoulders. 'This is violence!' Caesar cried, and at that moment one of Casca's brothers slipped behind and with a sweep of his dagger stabbed Caesar just below the throat. Confronted by a ring of drawn daggers, Caesar drew the top of his gown over his face. Twenty-three dagger thrusts went home as he stood there. Caesar was left lying dead until three of his slaves carried him home.

Julius Caesar's murderers had hoped to make the senate the centre of power once more. They failed. Immediately after Caesar's death there were more rivals for power: Mark Anthony and Gaius Octavius. Mark Anthony had been a friend of Caesar's. His speech at Caesar's funeral had been so moving that his murderers were forced to leave Rome. Gaius Octavius was Caesar's nephew (usually called Octavian by historians). He was determined to get revenge on his uncle's murderers. He did so and also became Rome's first emperor. The diagram on the next page will tell you more about him. Within twenty years the Roman Republic had finally come to an end and Rome was ruled by emperors.

How much power did the emperors have?

From 27 BC Rome had an emperor instead of a king. The first emperor preferred to call himself 'Princeps' (First Citizen), but there is no doubt that he had enormous power.

1 The emperor was Commander-in-Chief of the army. As long as he had the support of the army no-one could overthrow him.

2 He appointed almost all the officials in the city of Rome and so controlled the city.

3 He appointed all the governors in the provinces and so was able to make sure that only loyal men were given the jobs.

4 He was chief priest and in the eyes of many citizens was a god himself. Caligula (Emperor AD 37–41) actually declared himself a god.

5 The emperor had control over all the taxes paid to the Romans. He could therefore spend them in a way which made sure he remained popular. e.g. on bonuses to the army, or providing free bread for the citizens, or exciting gladiator shows.

509 BC Tarquinius Superbus, the last King of Rome, was driven out. Rome became a republic.

In 107 BC the Consul Marius opened up the army to all citizens. This meant that thousands of poorer Roman citizens could now join. The army started to become too big for the Consuls and Senate to control.

Mark Anthony fell in love with Cleopatra, the Queen of Egypt, in 41 BC. In 40 BC he was made to marry Octavian's sister, but he soon returned to Cleopatra. This made Octavian very angry.

27 BC Octavian was made Rome's first emperor, taking the name Augustus Caesar.

In 36 BC Lepidius tried to get more power. He was defeated by Octavian. In 31 BC Octavian defeated Mark Anthony in battle. He and Cleopatra committed suicide.

ROME HAS ITS FIRST FULL TIME ARMY. PEOPLE BEGIN TO WORRY!

59 BC

JULIUS CAESAR IN ELECTION VICTORY IS NOW CONSUL.

GAUL ROME

Julius Caesar and his Army return from conquering GAUL

SENATE WORRY HE'LL MAKE HIMSELF KING

RULES, RULES, RULES!

Julius Caesar was elected Consul in 59 BC and put in charge of the Roman army in Gaul. He returned in 49 BC having defeated all the tribes of Gaul. Caesar started behaving like a king, ignoring the senate, tribunes and assembly. In 44 BC a group of Senators tried to save the Republic by murdering Caesar.

43 BC

Mark Anthony and Octavian defeated Caesar's murderers. They, with the citizen Lepidius, divided the Empire between them. They became rivals.

MAP OF EMPIRE

CAESAR MURDERED 44 BC

SOMETHING MUST BE DONE!

SENATORS SAY

HE HAD TOO MUCH POWER!

Julius Caesar

Julius Caesar was born in about 102 BC. Like many important Romans, he rose to power through the army. As a general he led Roman armies into Gaul and Britain.

But Caesar wanted power. He was made dictator in 46 BC. This job was supposed to be temporary. When Caesar made himself dictator **for life** in 44 BC, he went too far. He was assassinated.

On 5 February AD 62 the Italian town of Pompeii was rocked by an earthquake. Almost all the buildings in the town were damaged and a flock of six hundred sheep is said to have been swallowed into a huge crack in the ground. After the earthquake the town was repaired and life returned to normal, but not for long.

Volcano!

Pompeii was built at the foot of the volcano, Mount Vesuvius. That volcano had been quiet for hundreds of years, but at midday on 24 August AD 79 it erupted.

The peak of the volcano flew 20 km into the air. Volcanic ash, pumice and rocks began to rain down on the terrified citizens of Pompeii.

Death and destruction

As the people tried to escape many of them were killed by poisonous gases which Vesuvius had thrown out. These people simply dropped to the ground and died where they lay. Ashes from the volcano continued to fall on them until they were completely covered under the 6 m layer which built up.

Source A

A painting of the destruction of Pompeii. It was painted by an English artist in 1820.

Source B

Pliny the Elder's nephew, the 18-year-old Younger Pliny saw the eruption from his uncle's villa at Misenum. He described what he had seen many years later.

Night came upon us, not like when the sky is cloudy, or when there is no moon, but like when you shut a room up and put all the lights out. You could hear the shrieks of women, the screams of children and the shouts of men. Some were calling for their children, others for their parents or their husbands and trying to recognise each other by the voices that replied.

Many cried over their fate, or the fate of their families; some lifting their hands to the gods. But most people were sure that there were now no gods at all, and that the final endless night of which we had heard had come upon the world.

Pompeii and the Bay of Naples.

Did anyone escape?

Some Pompeiians tried to escape by sea, but the eruption caused the sea to throw up huge waves which made it impossible to board boats. Archaeologists have found large numbers of skeletons at the water's edge, which probably shows how people tried unsuccessfully to leave by sea. One historian noticed that very few skeletons of horses have been found. He thinks that this may mean that some people escaped by riding to safety.

We don't know exactly how many people died at Pompeii, or in the neighbouring town of Herculaneum which was totally engulfed in boiling volcanic mud. We do know, however, that thousands of men, women and animals died a terrible death.

Among the dead was a Roman Admiral, Pliny the Elder. He lived in the town of Misenum, which was across the bay from Pompeii. His nephew tells us that when the eruption happened the wife of a friend in Pompeii sent a message asking him to rescue her. He set off, but was suffocated by the fumes before he could reach the town.

A buried city

After the eruption you could still see some of the columns of Pompeii's tallest buildings, but they were soon covered by drifting soil and grass. Soon all that was left of Pompeii was a large mound of earth.

Over 1500 years later (in 1594) workers building a water tunnel for a newly-built house cut through the remains of Pompeii. They thought that they had found a Roman villa and made no effort to investigate further.

It was not until 1748 that serious **excavations** began. Since then almost all of Pompeii and Herculaneum have been excavated.

Archaeologists have pieced together an outline of the city of Pompeii. It was over 64 hectares in area and had a town wall over 3 km long. It probably had a population of over 20,000. Streets were set out like a grid. In the centre of the town was a large forum (central square).

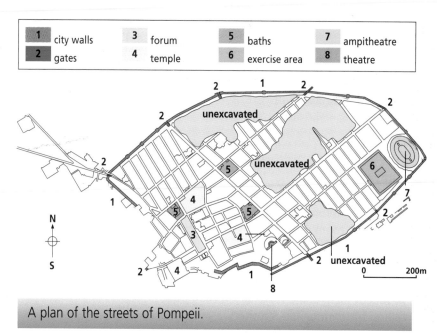

| 1 | city walls | 3 | forum | 5 | baths | 7 | ampitheatre |
| 2 | gates | 4 | temple | 6 | exercise area | 8 | theatre |

A plan of the streets of Pompeii.

The town also had many bath-houses, a sportsfield with swimming pool, two theatres and an **amphitheatre** which could hold up to 20,000 people. It was here that a riot took place in AD 59 and the amphitheatre was closed for ten years. A wall painting of the riot has survived the eruption.

Source C

A victim of Vesuvius, who died in the street.

A city full of people

Perhaps the saddest finds were the remains of humans. The volcanic ash covering the bodies had burned away the skin and the bodies rotted. But when the ash hardened it left a body-shaped hole. Archaeologists in the nineteenth century worked out that if they poured plaster into these cavities and left it to harden, they would have an exact copy of the dead person. They made plaster casts of many of the people of Pompeii.

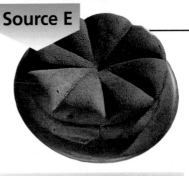

A loaf of bread from Pompeii. It looks perfect, but is rock hard!

Source D

The body of a dog found at Pompeii. The dog had been chained up outside its owner's house and had died struggling to get free.

Last moments

Not only can archaeologists work out what sort of people died, but also what they were doing when they died. Here are a few examples.

- A beggar with a new pair of shoes found on a street corner.
- Eighteen people huddled together in a cellar.
- At the gladiator's barracks a woman with a collection of fine jewels.
- A priest with an axe who had cut his way through the remains of a temple until the fumes overcame him.
- Two prisoners chained in one cell.
- Seven children killed when a baker's house collapsed.
- A family of four with the mother and father holding hands and the two children covered together.

Herculaneum

The town of Herculaneum is another victim of the volcano that hit Pompeii in AD 79.

We know more about Pompeii because it was larger and all of it has been excavated. Only a quarter of Herculaneum has been excavated. The rest of it is under the new town, which hangs on the edge of the excavations of the old town.

Pompeii was a commercial and industrial city. Herculaneum was a small market town and fishing port. There are grand houses in Herculaneum, the holiday homes of rich Romans who wanted to avoid the bustle of Pompeii.

There are things to see in Herculaneum that you cannot see in Pompeii. There is a complicated system of drains and sewers, with manhole covers in the street. The public baths are better preserved. One of the baths has fish painted all over it so that, filled with moving water, it would look as if fish were swimming in it! The changing rooms still have the shelves on the walls for the bathers to stack their clothes on.

A magnificent city

Shortly after Octavian became Emperor Augustus, he started a building programme in Rome which helped make the city one of the wonders of the world. Augustus wrote that he *found a city of bricks, but left a city of marble* and that he built *over 80 temples in the city*.

Over the next three hundred years many of the emperors built magnificent new buildings which amazed visitors to the city. Rome was so magnificent that it attracted thousands of people from the provinces who came to stare in wonder at the Colosseum, the Emperor's Palace, the Circus Maximus and the enormous numbers of temples, baths and gardens.

Luxury for everyone?

But what many of the visitors to Rome would not have seen was what life was like for most people who lived there. By the 1st century AD there were more than one million people living in Rome. Emperors were not that interested in housing for the poor in the city. Most ordinary Romans lived in cramped flats with no running water and no toilets. It has been estimated that for every wealthy person's town house there were 25 blocks of flats for 'ordinary citizens'.

For wealthy Romans life was very different. They lived in large town houses and had villas in the countryside where they went to avoid the crowds and the heat of the city.

Source A

The Roman writer Juvenal complaining about housing in Rome in the 1st century AD.

Most of the city is propped up with planks to stop it collapsing. Your landlord stands in front of cracks that have been there for years and says 'Sleep well!', although he knows that the house itself may not last the night.

I wish I lived where there were no fires, no midnight panics. Where I do not have to sleep next to the pigeon's nest, with only tiles between me and the rain.

A model of what historians think Rome would have looked like in AD 300.

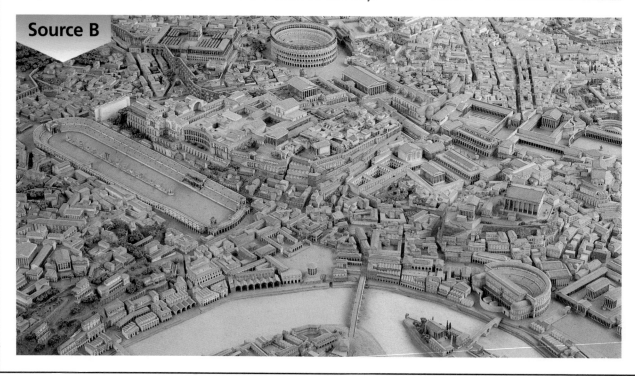

Source B

At the baths

The Romans loved a trip to the public baths. All large cities in the Empire had at least one public bath-house and of course wealthy Romans had their own baths in their villas.

The bath-house was a meeting place as well as a place for getting clean. At the baths you would meet your friends and catch up on the latest gossip. Both men and women went to the baths, though mixed bathing was generally frowned upon. Baths were cheap, and sometimes wealthy citizens would even 'sponsor' free days to make themselves popular with the local people.

Roman toilets

The Romans were much less squeamish about what they did in public than we are. Not only did they have public baths where they washed together, but they also had public toilets. Only rich people had their own private toilets. Public toilets might be a simple large jar, fastened to the wall of a building (and regularly emptied we hope) or a multi-seater public toilet where Romans would sit and chat as they went to the toilet. The Romans did not have toilet paper. Instead a supply of fresh water ran down the centre of the toilets and a sponge on a stick was provided instead of toilet paper. Once it had been used it was dipped into the water and passed on.

Source C

The Roman writer Seneca complaining about how he could not work in his room because of the noise from the local public baths.

My lodgings are right over a public bath house. It's enough to make a man hate his own ears. First there are the strenuous types exercising, swinging lead weights about in their hands, and grunting and groaning.

Then there are the less athletic types having a massage. All you hear is the slap of the hands on shoulders, or some fellow who likes singing in the bath, or the oafs who dive into the pool with the highest leaps and biggest splashes.

Source D

Source D

Unlike many paintings used as sources, Source D was not painted for decoration. It was painted specially for a book about the Romans, and its aim is to show exactly how Roman toilets worked.

A modern day postcard from the museum at Housesteads, a Roman fort on Hadrian's Wall in Britain. It shows soldiers using a communal toilet.

One of the most popular Roman entertainments was a day at the chariot races. In Rome there was a race track in the Circus Maximus which is believed to have held 250,000 spectators – though it has not survived. In the races up to twelve chariots, usually drawn by four horses, would race for seven laps around the track – about eight kilometres. Chariot drivers wore team colours and had supporters in the crowd, just as football teams do today. Often supporters carried banners and flags in their team colours and bet on their team.

Source A

A scene from the film *Ben Hur* showing a chariot race. This film was made in 1959.

The racing was very dangerous and there were frequent crashes (which the Romans called shipwrecks). Many charioteers were killed or badly injured. Successful charioteers earned a great deal of money. Since charioteers were usually slaves, most of the successful drivers used their winnings to buy their freedom.

The Games

Another very popular form of entertainment were 'the Games'. These took place in the Colosseum and were a spectacle of killing.

In the morning there were animal shows. These might just be displays of trained animals performing tricks, but they would soon turn more violent. Starved animals would be matched against each other, or would be hunted in the arena and then slaughtered. When the Emperor Trajan had special Games to celebrate his victory in war 11,000 animals died.

Source B

Not everyone enjoyed the chariot races. This was written by a Roman nobleman, complaining about them:

Yes the races are on – and they don't interest me at all. When you've seen one you've seen them all. If it were the speed of the horses or the skill of the drivers that attracted the spectators, there would be some point in it.

But it's only the colours worn by the drivers they go to see. If the drivers changed shirts the crowd would change with them, abandoning the driver they had cheered so hard for before.

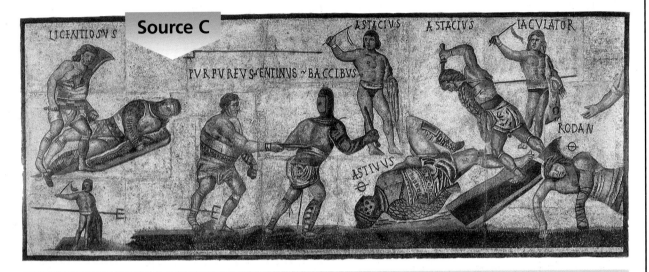

Source C

A Roman mosaic showing gladiators fighting.

Most exciting for the spectators were the fights between animals like lions and tigers, and humans. Sometimes the humans had weapons, but criminals usually had to fight without weapons, and were bound to die.

After midday it was time for the gladiator fights. Gladiators were criminals, captured prisoners of war or slaves who trained to fight each other to the death.

Spared by the crowd?

There were three types of gladiator. *Samnites* had a large shield and a protective **visor**. *Thracians* had lighter armour and just a small sword. The poor *Retarius* had to defend himself with just a net, a dagger and a **trident**. If a gladiator was wounded he would raise his finger, asking for mercy. If his fighting had pleased the crowd, he would be spared. If not, his opponent killed him. Some gladiators won many fights and earned enough to buy their freedom. Usually it was just a matter of time before a gladiator was killed. When the Colosseum was opened in AD 80 there was a special Games lasting for 100 days. Over 1000 gladiators died.

Source D

A Roman writer criticising what he has seen at the Games:

'Kill!' they shout. 'Beat him! Burn him! Why won't he face the sword? What a coward! Why can't he die more eagerly? Beat his wounded back – they must strike each other's bare chest! Oh – it's the interval. Well let's have someone strangled: we must have <u>something</u> to watch.'

Spartacus

Spartacus was born in Thrace. He was brought to Rome as a prisoner of war. He was made a slave and forced to train as a gladiator.

In 73 BC Spartacus led a slave revolt in Italy. Huge numbers of slaves joined the revolt. At its biggest, Spartacus's army could have had as many as 90,000 men in it. They defeated two armies sent against them by the Roman government and rampaged around southern Italy.

They went on winning. In 73 BC they beat three more armies and marched up into northern Italy. They were not beaten until 71 BC. Spartacus died in battle. All those who were captured were crucified.

Wealthy Romans often owned a house in the country as well as one in the town. The country house was called a villa. It was a place to escape from the bustle of the city, but often it had another function too. It was the farmhouse in an estate where slaves and **tenants** worked the land and helped produce the crops which bought their master's wealth. A well-run villa could make its owner money. It also gave him food and drink, so he did not have to buy as much at market. He could also make money by selling any extra crops he had.

Villas were usually decorated with expensive floor or wall **mosaics** and many had their own form of central heating called a **hypocaust**. This wood-burning furnace produced hot air which travelled under a raised floor, up through channels in the walls. The floor was held up by small pillars. You can see a picture of a hypocaust on page 45.

What did they eat?

The owners of the villa and their guests led comfortable lives. They ate three meals a day, though the first two were very light. Breakfast was just a snack, like bread and honey. At mid-morning came another snack, like bread and cheese. The main meal was eaten late in the afternoon. If the family was alone then they ate wheatmeal porridge flavoured with herbs or cheese. But, if a wealthy family was entertaining important guests then they would eat a meal with as many as eight courses. This could contain a variety of dishes, such as pheasant, partridge or even dormouse.

Where did they eat?

The meal was not eaten around a table, but on couches. People ate in a half-lying position scooping up food with bread or their fingers. They did not use knives and forks. People who were full sometimes left the room to make themselves vomit, then came back and carried on eating.

Who else lived in the countryside?

Of course, the vast majority of country people were not wealthy and living in villas. Instead most people lived in houses which were much simpler. Historians have found it difficult to find out about these houses as almost nothing has survived of them. Also, Roman writers did not generally tell us about ordinary people, as they thought their lives were too dull. We believe, however, that their houses were small and round with thatched roofs. The centre of the roof would have a hole for the smoke to escape. The floor would not be covered with expensive mosaics, but instead would be hard-beaten earth.

An ordinary meal

Unlike the wealthy villa owner, the ordinary country people had a diet based almost entirely upon wheat which was boiled to make a kind of porridge. This would be flavoured with sauces and vegetables or, much more rarely, fish or meat. Meat was very expensive and even rich families did not always have it in their meals.

Cogidubnus

Cogidubnus ruled a British tribe based at Chichester. When the Romans invaded, he decided to co-operate with them. He hoped that if he did this they would let him carry on ruling. They did. He was given Roman citizenship and a Roman name – Tiberius Claudius Cogidubnus.

This is almost all we know about him. He is believed to have lived at the Roman villa at Fishbourne, the grandest yet found in Britain.

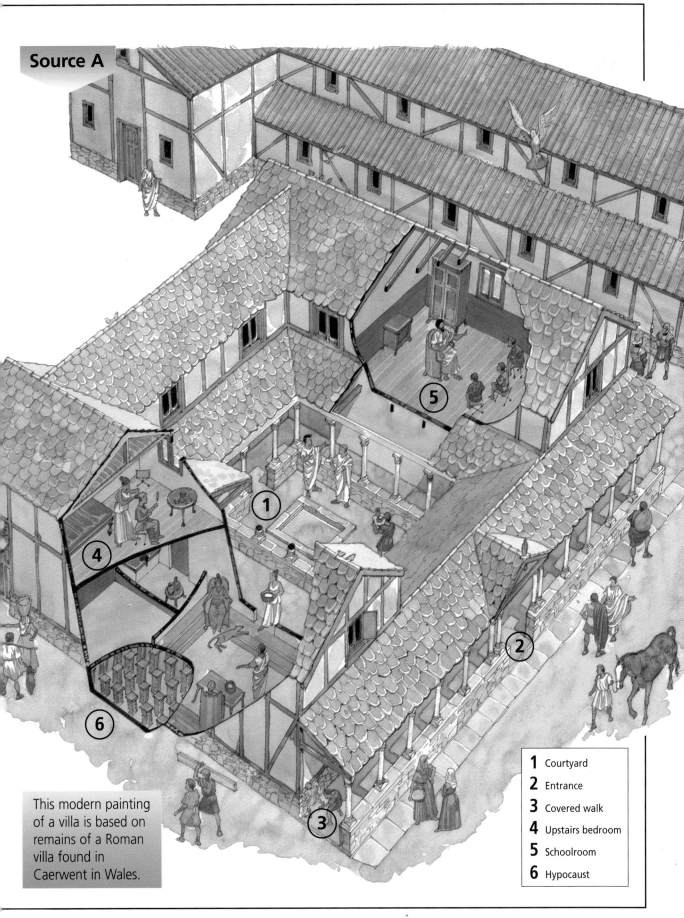

Source A

1 Courtyard
2 Entrance
3 Covered walk
4 Upstairs bedroom
5 Schoolroom
6 Hypocaust

This modern painting of a villa is based on remains of a Roman villa found in Caerwent in Wales.

A very popular pastime for the Romans was a trip to the public baths. Wealthy Romans had their own set of baths in their villas, like the one shown here. Inside these bath-houses were a number of rooms, each designed to make a visit to the baths an enjoyable as well as a healthy one.

Source A

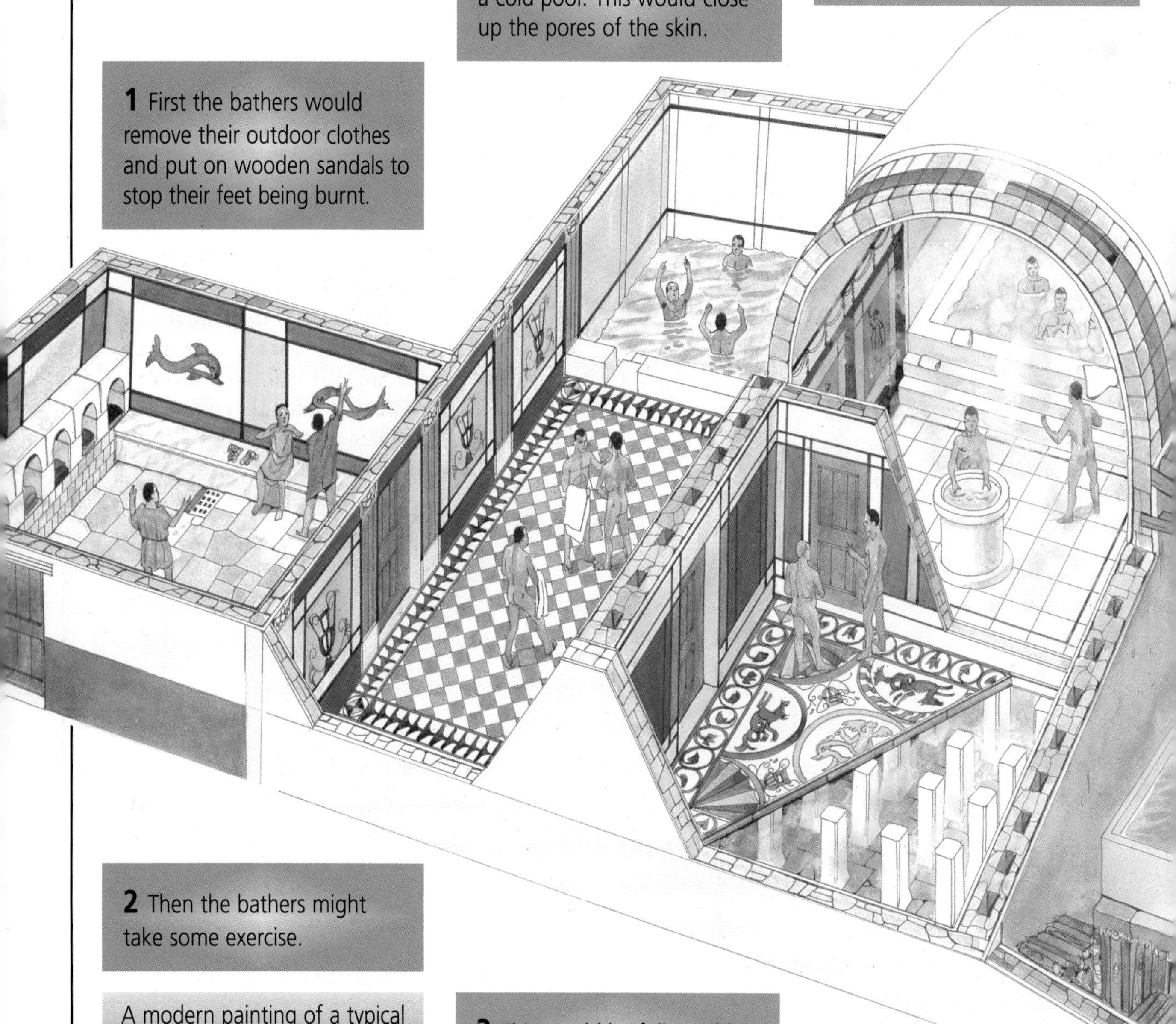

4 Then came the hot steam room (one Roman writer once described such a room as *like being on a bonfire*). Here bathers would clean themselves by rubbing perfumed oil into their skin. As they sweated they would rub off the oil using a scraper called a *strigil*.

5 To finish the visit, the bathers would plunge into a cold pool. This would close up the pores of the skin.

1 First the bathers would remove their outdoor clothes and put on wooden sandals to stop their feet being burnt.

2 Then the bathers might take some exercise.

A modern painting of a typical Roman bath-house. Note the hypocaust furnace outside the main building.

3 This would be followed by a visit to the warm room.

Roman fashions

In Roman times men would generally be clean-shaven. Shaving was considered too difficult to do yourself so it was done either by a slave or by visiting the barber regularly. The poor could not afford this and so had stubble or short beards. Some men were very concerned about losing their hair, and used lots of potions to try to stop going bald. One such potion was made from rat droppings!

Women changed their hairstyles to follow the fashion of the time, and some women wore wigs to create new hairstyles. There were also a large number of cosmetics which wealthy women could use. These ranged from face creams made with milk and flour to expensive imported Indian scents.

Ovid

Ovid was born in about 43 BC. He went to Rome to train to be a lawyer, but became a writer instead. He is famous for his love poems. He was exiled in 8 BC. The reason the Emperor Augustus gave for this was that Ovid's latest poems, *Ars Amatoria*, were immoral. Some say he was involved with the Emperor's daughter, Julia.

Source B

The remains of the hypocaust from Chedworth Roman villa.

Source C

The Roman writer Ovid, feeling sorry for men losing their hair.

There is nothing graceful about becoming bald. Snatched by age, our hairs fall out like autumn leaves torn by a cold wind from the trees. When a woman's hair turns white, she dyes it with German herbs and makes her hair a better colour than her natural colour.

Source D

The Roman poet, Martial complaining about his barber. He wrote this in the 1st century AD.

He who does not wish to descend to the underworld should avoid the barber Antiochus. These scars on my chin may look like those on a boxer's face, but I did not get them from boxing, nor from the sharp nails of a fierce wife. Instead they came from the accursed steel [blade] and hand of Antiochus.

Source E

A poem written by the Roman poet, Martial, in the 1st century AD.

You live at home, Galla, but not your beauty – that lives at the chemist's. Your hair was made in far away Germany, and your teeth are put away in boxes just like your dresses. When you get into bed the rest of you is boxed up in a hundred little boxes – even your face sleeps somewhere else.

Roman family life was dominated by men. The man was head of the household and expected obedience from his wife and family. The Romans called him the *paterfamilias* (father of the household). However, recent research into Roman families has shown that in general men married at a much later age than women. This meant that many fathers died before their children grew up, as the life expectancy for a man in Roman times was 25 years. So it has been estimated that up to a third of Roman children may have lived in a family where the father had died before they reached the age of ten.

Women and childbirth

Although wealthy women might have the money to buy expensive potions and perfumes to cover ageing, it was a sad fact of Roman life that enormous numbers of women did not reach what we consider to be old age. The average life expectancy for women was just 28 years (today in Britain it is nearly 79). A major cause of this was probably the dangers of childbirth. Women could legally marry at the age of 12 and there are many records of wives who were married when they were in their teens. Since there were no effective methods of contraception many women had large numbers of children and were pregnant or recovering from pregnancy for much of their adult life.

After birth a child would be inspected by the midwife. If it was not healthy it would probably be left to die. Even if it was healthy it might not survive. Quite often the father made the decision to allow female babies to die because girls were not valued as highly as boys.

Roman children played with similar toys to us. This rag doll from Roman times was found in Egypt.

Children

After birth on the eighth or ninth day a child was named and was ready for life. What happened then depended on how rich the family was. A child from a poor family would be looked after by its mother and as soon as he or she was old enough would be expected to go out to work. In some cases fathers sold their children to wealthy Romans to be slaves.

The life of a rich child was very different. His or her mother would have slaves to help bring up the child who might have a variety of expensive toys to play with. Archaeologists have found remains of dolls' houses, see-saws, rocking horses and dolls in Ancient Rome. Girls would be taught the skills required to be good housewives, whereas boys would be encouraged in more physical activities, such as running and throwing spears. This would help them prepare for life in the army.

Children of rich families started school at the age of seven. Discipline was strict. Caning on the hand was common and more serious bad behaviour was punished by flogging with a leather whip. The lessons generally started at dawn and continued until noon. Often the same teacher would give the children lessons in reading, writing and arithmetic. Once this had been learned children moved on to study grammar and literature. But since the majority of Romans were poor and did not attend school, most children grew up unable to read and write.

Source B

VICTIMS OF ANCIENT FAMILY PLANNING UNEARTHED IN MASS BABIES' GRAVE

Scientists have found a mass grave of more than 100 babies – all only one or two days old – in a Roman settlement in fourth century Israel. Theya Molleson of the Natural History Museum in London was not surprised by the find: 'The practice of allowing babies to die was a totally normal practice throughout the Roman world. It was straightforward population control. They didn't have the ready access to contraception that we have, so the decision was made later, once the baby was born,' she said.

Extract from The *Guardian* newspaper 16 January 1997.

Cruel parents?

Source B suggests that people allowed unwanted babies to die. The Greeks also left them to die, as did the Chinese, and probably others did too. At this time many babies, and mothers, died in childbirth or from later infection. Newborn babies dying was much more common than it is today.

We must also remember that the Romans had less access to contraception. What they had to use was not very effective. Families could not always afford their new babies. To many Romans it might have seemed kinder to allow a newborn baby to die if they were short of money. It meant they would be better able to care for the children they already had.

Who did the work?

One of the things which some people criticise about Ancient Rome was its widespread use of slaves. By the 1st century AD there were about 400,000 slaves in Rome. This was enough for each family to have two of their own – though most Romans were too poor to have any slaves.

Bought and sold

When the Romans conquered new lands they would take some of the people to be slaves. These people were sold in market-places in Rome as if they were animals. The price of the slave depended upon his or her skills. A strong, fit, male slave would be valuable to work on his owner's land, or to join a gang of slaves owned by a contractor who built roads and bridges. Other slaves were used to clean the house, keep the garden tidy, cook the food or help the woman of the house with her make-up and dress. The slaves on sale in the market place often included very well-educated people. The Greeks provided large numbers of clever slaves. The Romans used these slaves as doctors, teachers, librarians, or to run the household accounts.

A hard life?

Some slaves were treated harshly by their masters. Others had a better standard of living than they would have had if they had been free. But they could be sold at any time and always had to obey their master's or mistress's orders. Runaway slaves were severely punished as a warning to other slaves. If a slave murdered his master, then all of the slaves in the household were put to death, as shown in the story of Pedanius Secundus. After Pedanius was murdered in AD 61, all 400 of his slaves were condemned to death. There was so much opposition to the killing of innocent children and old people that the matter was discussed in the Senate. There it was decided that the punishment should still be carried out.

Sometimes owners set slaves free as a reward. These people became 'freedmen'. They could own property, but could not vote and were not Roman citizens. The children of freedmen were, however, Roman citizens.

Source A

A Roman mosaic of a boy slave.

Source B

A rich nobleman praising a fellow Roman for the way he treats his slaves.

Your recent visitors tell me how friendly you are with your slaves. This pleases me. People will object and say 'They're only slaves!' Maybe, but they are human beings like ourselves, and I would rather call them friends – humble friends.

A Roman statue of the god Mars.

The main Roman gods

Apollo:	The god of the sun and prophecy
Diana:	The goddess of the moon and hunting
Jupiter:	The king of the gods
Juno:	The queen of the gods
Mars:	The god of war
Mercury:	The messenger of the gods
Neptune:	The god of the sea
Venus:	The goddess of love

Which gods did the Romans believe in?

The Romans had a large number of their own gods, but often added other gods. For example, when they conquered Greece they took the twelve main Greek gods and gave them Roman names.

The Romans thought that each individual family had its own **specia** – gods who looked after them. So it was quite common to see a small shrine at the house entrance or in the corner of the room.

The Romans built temples to their many gods and there were festivals on special days for each god. Sacrifices were made by the priests who thought that they could read messages from the gods by examining the insides of dead animals. It seems a little strange that such practical people as the Romans thought that they could predict success or failure in battle by the size of a dead goat's liver!

One of the new religions which the Romans first met in Palestine in the 1st century AD was Christianity. Since Christians believed that their god was the only god and they would not worship Roman gods, their religion was banned by the emperor. In 64 AD they were accused of having burned Rome down and according to Tacitus a group of them were put to death by *being covered in animal skins and torn to death by dogs, or were nailed to crosses and set alight when evening came.*

Christians continued their worship in secret and thousands of them were captured and killed fighting wild animals in the Colosseum in Rome. But slowly their religion spread and in the fourth century AD the Emperor Constantine (306–337 AD) even became a Christian. Once the emperor took on a religion it became very fashionable and many Romans changed to it too. In AD 380 Emperor Theodosius made Christianity the official religion of the Empire and banned other religions.

Slaves

Slaves were not just house servants, or farm workers. They did all sorts of jobs. Many slaves kept their owners' records and accounts. Some were school teachers. Some slaves, especially Greek slaves, were even doctors. A list of doctors in Rome from AD 1 to AD 300 shows about 75% of all doctors were Greek slaves.

7.1 WHY DID CAESAR INVADE BRITAIN?

The Romans did not begin to take over Britain until the year AD 43. But that did not mean that they had not been there before. In fact, a Roman army had been sent to Britain almost a hundred years earlier.

Why invade?

The first army was led by Julius Caesar. At the time of his invasion he was in charge of the Roman army in Gaul (modern-day France). The Gauls were hard people to control and Caesar knew that some of his enemies in Gaul had help from 'the Britons'. It was time that the Britons were taught a thing or two about the power of the Roman army. That way they might learn to behave themselves.

But there were other reasons for Caesar's invasion. He was involved in disputes with other generals in Rome (see page 31). If he could defeat the British he would gain more support. Britain also had valuable trade goods such as tin and pearls.

The invasion

Caesar's troops came to Britain in August, 55 BC. They had intended to land at Richborough in Kent, but Caesar saw that the Britons would be able to attack his troops from the cliffs overlooking the beach. So he sailed up the coast to Deal. Even there his troops did not seem very keen to land (read Source B)! Once they were ashore Caesar's army advanced inland. They captured hostages before a storm damaged their ships. After repairing them, the Romans sailed back to Gaul.

Back again

Caesar returned in the next year, 54 BC, with a much larger force. This time he met little resistance on the beach and advanced over 100 miles inland. He defeated the leading British chief, Cassivellaunus in battle. Caesar took hostages and money from the British. Then he went back to Gaul, saying he left *for fear of a sudden uprising in Gaul* whilst so many troops were away. We don't know if this was the real reason. Perhaps conquering all of Britain looked like it was more trouble than it was worth.

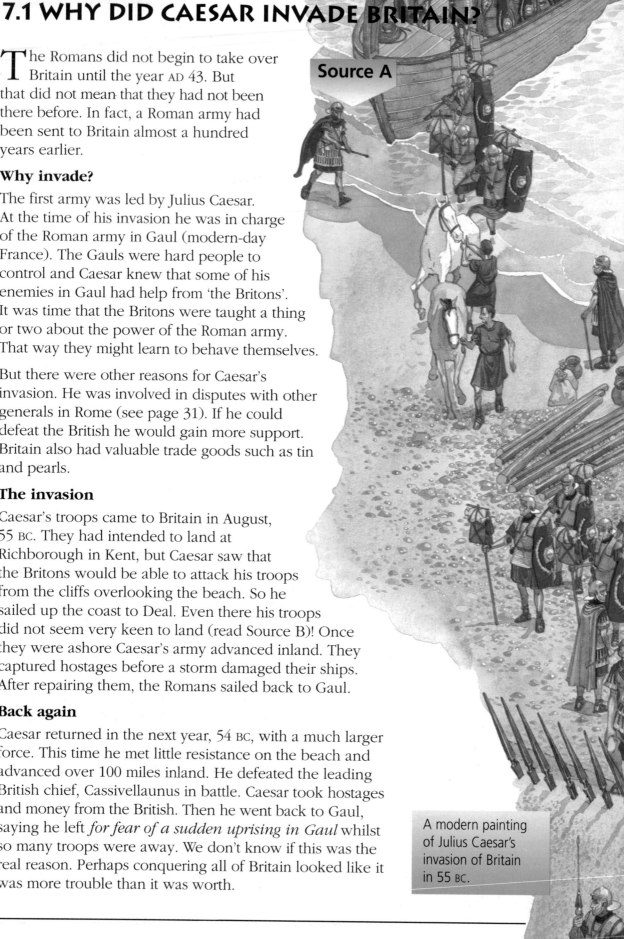

Source A

A modern painting of Julius Caesar's invasion of Britain in 55 BC.

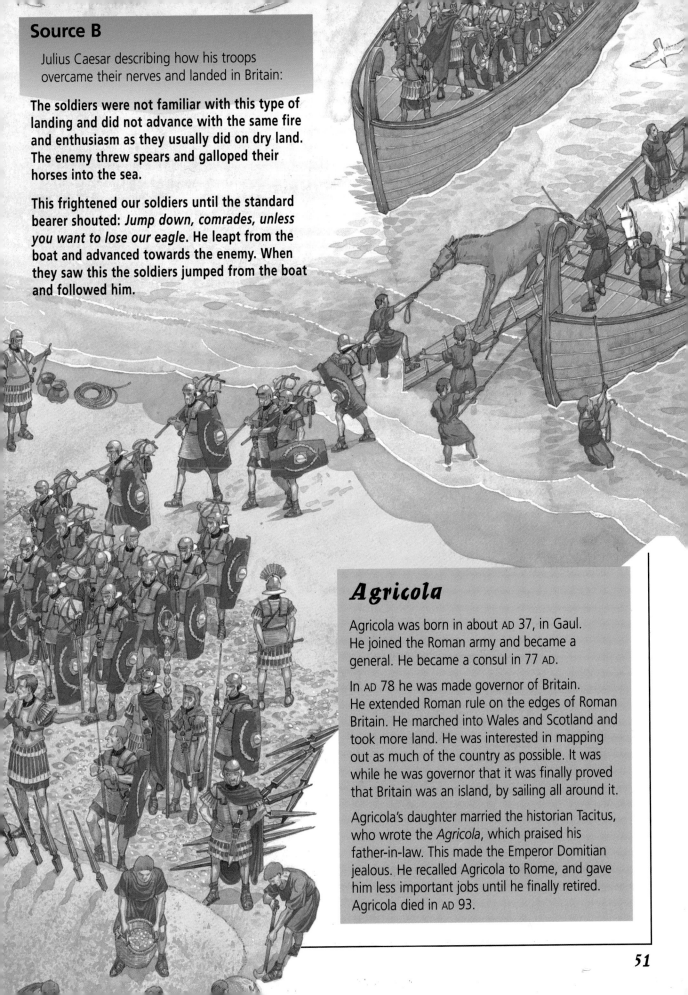

Julius Caesar describing how his troops overcame their nerves and landed in Britain:

The soldiers were not familiar with this type of landing and did not advance with the same fire and enthusiasm as they usually did on dry land. The enemy threw spears and galloped their horses into the sea.

This frightened our soldiers until the standard bearer shouted: *Jump down, comrades, unless you want to lose our eagle.* He leapt from the boat and advanced towards the enemy. When they saw this the soldiers jumped from the boat and followed him.

Agricola

Agricola was born in about AD 37, in Gaul. He joined the Roman army and became a general. He became a consul in 77 AD.

In AD 78 he was made governor of Britain. He extended Roman rule on the edges of Roman Britain. He marched into Wales and Scotland and took more land. He was interested in mapping out as much of the country as possible. It was while he was governor that it was finally proved that Britain was an island, by sailing all around it.

Agricola's daughter married the historian Tacitus, who wrote the *Agricola*, which praised his father-in-law. This made the Emperor Domitian jealous. He recalled Agricola to Rome, and gave him less important jobs until he finally retired. Agricola died in AD 93.

Caesar had not conquered Britain, just shown enough force to warn the Britons not to side with the Gauls against Rome. By AD 43 the Romans had decided to bring Britain into their Empire, particularly as the Britons were still causing trouble in Gaul. The Emperor, Claudius, had only been ruling for two years. Conquering Britain would help to convince people that he was a strong ruler.

So Claudius sent Aulus Plautius, one of his best generals, to Britain with 40,000 soldiers. The invasion got off to a very bad start. Some of the soldiers thought that the English Channel marked the end of the civilised world and that unknown horrors were waiting in Britain for them. Eventually the army set off and landed at Richborough on the Kent coast. Aulus Plautius fought his way across south-east Britain until he reached Colchester. This was the base of the leading British tribe, the Catuvallauni. Their leader Caractacus had already been defeated and had fled to Wales. Plautius knew he could capture the town. He sent to Rome for the Emperor. Claudius wanted to be involved in the victory.

An imperial victory

Claudius arrived in Britain in mid-August. He rode through the centre of Colchester on an elephant. Several British leaders surrendered to him. He made Plautius governor of Britain and returned to Rome to celebrate the capture of Britain. Claudius' two-year-old son was renamed Britannicus.

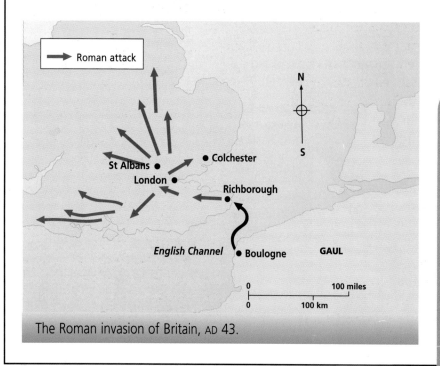

The Roman invasion of Britain, AD 43.

Source A

The Romans finally captured the Catuvellauni leader, Caractacus. He was sent to Rome to be shown off and then executed. But Claudius was so impressed by Caractacus' speech (recorded by Tacitus, below) that he was allowed to live.

I had horses, men, arms and wealth. Are you surprised I am sorry to lose them? If I had surrendered without a blow before being brought to you, your victory would not look so great. If you execute me, your glory will soon be forgotten. But if you spare me I shall be an everlasting example of your mercy.

THE HEAD OF CLAUDIUS

In the spring of 1907, a boy swimming in the River Alde in Suffolk spotted something odd stuck in the river bed. He dived down to see what it was, and pulled out this bronze head of Claudius! It is now displayed in the British Museum, London. The jagged edges around the neck suggest that it was violently hacked from the body of the statue during Boudica's revolt of AD 60.

Maiden Castle in Dorset. It had a series of fortified defences, but was still captured by the Roman army led by General Vespasian. Later he became one of Rome's emperors.

Did all of Britain become Roman?

After Claudius left, Plautius continued the advance into Britain and soon the whole of eastern and southern Britain was under Roman control. However, the Romans found the conquest of the rest of Britain much more difficult. Northern and western Britain is hilly and much harder to fight in. But the conquest of Britain continued, despite several serious set backs (see page 54).

The edge of conquest

In AD 117 it was decided to build a wall across Britain separating the Roman province in the south from the uncivilised north. This was Hadrian's Wall. In AD 142 a further wall was built across Scotland (the Antonine Wall), but it lasted only forty years before the Romans retreated once more to Hadrian's Wall. This remained the limit of Rome's Empire in Britain for the next two hundred years.

Claudius

Claudius was born in Gaul in 10 BC. He suffered from ill health and a stammer. Because of this, he did not become a politician, but studied and wrote books.

Claudius was the nephew of Tiberius, who became Emperor in AD 14. At this time there was a lot of plotting at the Imperial court, and many people who might have been used by the army to replace Tiberius were exiled or killed. Claudius was allowed to stay, because he was seen as harmless.

In AD 41 the army murdered the mad Emperor Caligula and made Claudius emperor. He died in AD 54. It was said that his wife poisoned him.

7.3 DID BOUDICA'S REVOLT REALLY WORRY THE ROMANS?

In AD 60 the governor of Britain, Suetonius Paulinus, took his legions into Wales to attack the Druids there. While he was away there was a rebellion of British tribes against the Romans.

The rebellion was led by the widow of Prasutagus, King of the Iceni. He had just died and left his kingdom jointly to his wife Boudica and the Emperor Nero. But the Romans tried to take the kingdom just for themselves. Tacitus tells us what happened next. His words are in *italics*:

Prasutagus had hoped by making the emperor his joint ruler that he would be able to stop his kingdom being attacked. But it turned out otherwise. His kingdom was attacked, his widow Boudica flogged and his daughters raped. The King's own relatives were treated like slaves.

This behaviour led to a massive uprising by the British. Of course most of the people involved didn't really care what had happened to Boudica. They were just trying to get rid of the Romans.

Led by Queen Boudica, the rebellious British troops attacked Colchester, then burned down London and St. Albans. Up to 70,000 Romans and their British friends were slaughtered. Tacitus tells us that:

The Britons made for where there was most to steal and where Roman defences were weakest. They could not wait to cut throats, hang, burn and crucify.

Paulinus was forced to rush back from Wales to deal with the rebellion. He collected together all the soldiers he could, but his army was still only 10,000 strong. Boudica's army had nearly 120,000 men. Boudica and her army must have looked frighteningly strong to the Romans. But the Roman armies were too powerful for the British. A slaughter followed with enormous British losses.

Boudica took poison and was soon dead. She did not want the Romans to capture her and parade her as another defeated British leader.

Source A

Some modern artists have tried to draw what they think Boudica looked like.

Source B

The Roman writer, Cassius Dio, describes Boudica:

She was huge and frightening to look at with a mass of ginger hair that hung to her knees. Her voice was as harsh as she looks. She dressed in a multi-coloured tunic with a thick cloak fastened by a brooch flung over it, and wore a heavy gold necklace. She shook a spear to terrify all who watched her.

Boudica: what's in a name?

The name Boudica has been famously misspelt throughout history. The Roman historian, Tacitus, was the first to get it wrong by giving the name two 'c's - Boudicca. Then someone copying a manuscript in the Middle Ages mistook the 'u' for an 'a' and the second 'c' for an 'e', making Boadicea. The Victorians continued to misspell it this way! We know now how it is supposed to be spelt, because the name Boudica appears on many inscriptions made long before Tacitus wrote.

Source C

On the side of the Thames in London is this statue. Note the fierce spikes sticking out of the side of Boudica's chariot!

Source D

Before the battle Boudica made a moving speech to her army, reported here by Tacitus:

We British are used to woman commanders in war. I am descended from mighty men. I am fighting for my lost freedom, my bruised body and my outraged daughters. The gods will grant us the revenge we deserve. The Romans will never face even the noise made by all our thousands, let alone the strength of our attack.

Source E

Tacitus describes the British losses:

According to one report almost 80, 000 Britons fell. Our own casualties were about 400 dead and a slightly larger number of wounded.

Tacitus

Tacitus was born in about AD 55. We do not know much about his early life. He probably came from southern France or northern Italy.

Tacitus came to Rome and became a senator. He married the daughter of the famous general, Agricola, in AD 77. He was made a consul in AD 97. In about AD 112 he was made Governor of the province of Asia.

Tacitus was not just a successful politician. He also wrote books. He wrote about education and about different peoples of the Empire. He wrote a book in praise of his father-in-law that got Agricola into trouble! But he is most famous for his two sets of history books about the history of Rome, *Histories* and *Annals*. Both of these had over ten volumes in them, although not all of them have survived to the present day. His books give a very biased account of the various rulers of Rome from AD 14 to AD 96.

Source A

The Roman Wall near Housesteads in Northumberland, photographed in recent times.

A final frontier?

In the year AD 117 tribes in Scotland and northern England attacked the Romans and caused widespread destruction. Shortly after, Emperor Hadrian visited Britain. He decided that he would need a huge army to conquer Scotland. And it would be hard to keep it. Hadrian thought it would make more sense to build a wall separating the tribes of Scotland from those of northern England. Hadrian said the wall would *separate the Romans and the barbarians.*

The Emperor chose to build the wall across the narrowest part of Britain from what is now Wallsend on Tyne in the east to Bowness on Solway in the west.

A well-built wall

The Romans used soldiers, who were excellent builders, to build the wall. It probably took at least five years to build. Each of the legions in the area was given sections about 8 kms long to build. Once each section was finished an inscribed stone was added to show who had built it.

Hadrian's Wall acted as an effective barrier against attacks from Scottish tribes for over 250 years (though it had to be rebuilt three times). Much of Hadrian's Wall still survives today – despite the fact that roads, churches and even private houses in the area used stones from the wall for building work!

There were five different parts to the frontier around Hadrian's Wall.

1 The wall itself was about 3 m wide and was built from stone quarried in the area. Over a million cubic metres of stone were needed to build the wall. Not surprisingly, there was a shortage of stone. A central stretch of the wall was built in turf, though later it was rebuilt in stone. The Romans built the wall so that anyone attacking it from the north would have to climb uphill.

2 On the northern side of the wall there was a ditch, 9 m wide and almost 4 m deep. Any attackers would have to cross this ditch before getting to the wall.

3 Another ditch or **vallum**, less wide and deep, was built on the south, 'friendly', side of the wall. Modern historians believe that it acted as a boundary line. Any Briton crossing the vallum without permission was a potential enemy.

4 All along the wall, about 8 km apart, were forts for about 500 men. They contained workshops, foodstores, barracks and hospitals.

5 Between the forts, about 1500 m apart, were milecastles, which held 100 men. Finally, between each milecastle were two turrets where two or three men stood guard; ready to signal to the milecastle and forts if an attack began.

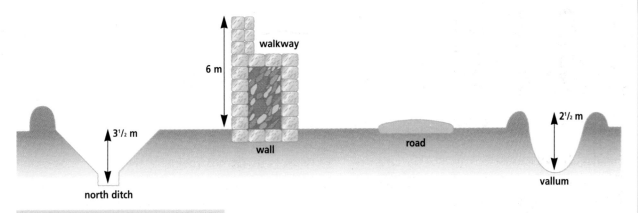

A diagram of the Roman Wall.

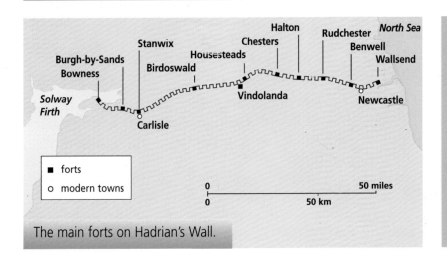

The main forts on Hadrian's Wall.

Forts

The forts along the wall varied in comfort and size. Most of them had civilian settlements outside the gates. The families of the soldiers lived here, as well as British traders and retired soldiers. Most forts had baths. Larger ones, such as Housesteads, had temples too.

7.5 VINDOLANDA – 'A TREASURE TROVE OF ROMAN HISTORY'

Just a few miles south of Hadrian's Wall is the fort of Vindolanda. The first fort on the site was built in AD 85, and over the next 300 years troops from many different Roman provinces were stationed there.

In modern times Vindolanda has been an important site for historians of Roman Britain. Many **artefacts** or old objects have been found there and we have learned much about the Roman way of life.

The most dramatic finds occurred in the early 1970s. Archaeologists digging at the site began to find documents written on wooden tablets.

These documents were obviously badly decayed, but it has been possible to preserve much of what was written.

What did the documents say?

We now have fragments of over 250 written documents. The archaeologists were very excited by the discovery of these tablets as they are the first ever documents written by soldiers that we have found in Britain. They tell us that, at a time when very few people around the world could read or write, many Roman soldiers were writing letters to their friends and relatives.

Source A

Source B

A list of food and drink mentioned in the Vindolanda tablets:

Wine, garlic, fish, pork, cereal, butter, deer, beer, spices, beans, goat, barley, lentils, honey, olives, oysters, eggs, bread, ham, plums, chicken, radishes, salt, pepper, semolina.

A reconstruction in the Vindolanda Museum of what a Roman kitchen may have looked like.

Source C

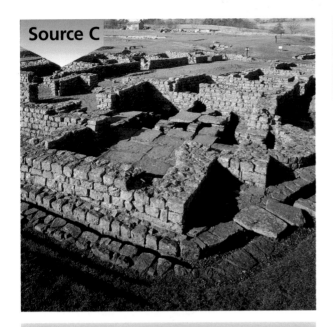

The remains of buildings at Vindolanda.

Source D

A pendant found at Vindolanda.

Source E

A child's sandal found at Vindolanda.

Source F

Extracts from some of the Vindolanda tablets.

FROM CLAUDIA SEVERA TO SULPICIA LEPIDINA:

Greetings to Lepidina, on the third day before the Ides of September. I give you a warm invitation for the day of the celebration of my birthday. Make sure that you come to us, to make the day more enjoyable for me.

APPEAL FOR MERCY:

I implore your majesty not to allow me, an innocent man, to be beaten with rods. I beg you not to allow an innocent man to be bloodied by rods as if he had committed some crime.

SOLEMIS TO HIS BROTHER, PARIS:

I send you greetings brother. I want you to know that I am in very good health, as I hope you are. You have been very bad about writing. I have not received a single letter from you. But, of course, I am a much more considerate person so I am writing to you.

John Collingwood-Bruce

John Collingwood-Bruce was born in 1805 in Newcastle-upon-Tyne. He thought of becoming a preacher, but in the end became a teacher instead. He taught in a private school, owned by his father, which he later inherited.

Collingwood-Bruce was fascinated by the Romans and Hadrian's Wall. He visited the wall each year, investigating different places all along it. He drew maps of different parts of the wall. In 1851 and 1886 he organized 'pilgrimage' trips there.

Collingwood-Bruce wrote articles and books on the wall, too. One of the most famous was *The Roman Wall*, published in 1851. He belonged to several societies for studying archaeology. He was married, with two sons and two daughters. He died in 1892, aged 87.

The end of the Roman Empire

The Roman Empire had been built up over a period of hundreds of years. It came to an end in a similar way. People did not wake up and say. 'That's the end of the Roman Empire, then'. Instead, over a period of time more and more places which had been under Roman rule were taken over by local tribes.

On page 17 you saw that the Empire had been divided to make it easier to run. But by the beginning of the 5th century AD both Empires came under attack from tribes such as the Franks, the Vandals, the Huns and the Visigoths. In AD 410 and again in AD 455 these tribes captured Rome and stole many of its valuable treasures. Soon Roman rule in the west had come to an end.

The eastern empire, called the Byzantine Empire because its capital was Byzantium, continued for much longer. Eventually in 1453 it was captured by the Muslims and the eastern empire came to an end.

What did the Romans leave us?

The Romans had ruled most of Europe for over three hundred years, so when their Empire collapsed in the west it did not mean that people suddenly stopped being influenced by Roman ideas. Their rule had a lasting effect. Historians call this the **Legacy of Rome**. It can be seen in many areas. Here are some examples.

Language

Latin, the language of the Romans, was used for official business throughout the Empire. After the Empire ended it continued to be used in church services and as the language in which government business was done. The Latin language has also influenced the languages of many other Europe languages. Even today in Britain many of our words can be dated back to the time of the Romans and Latin is still taught in some schools today.

Literature and ideas

The Romans had a large number of talented writers and many of their books survived after the Empire fell. Monks in monasteries continued to write in Latin and to study Latin writers.

Latin words surviving today

English words
Decimal
Magistrate
Naval
Principal
Science
Table
Video

Latin words
Decem meaning ten
Magister meaning a teacher
Navis meaning a ship
Princeps meaning a chief
Scio meaning I know
Tabula meaning a board
Video meaning I see

The Arch of Titus, built in AD 81 to celebrate Roman victory in Palestine.

Source A

Then, in the fifteenth century during the time of the **Renaissance**, many educated people outside the monasteries became fascinated by the Roman way of life. They began to study Latin so that they could read Roman writers. They also began to copy Roman art, write in a Roman style and discuss Roman ideas on medicine and architecture.

Christianity

At first the Romans had tried to stamp out Christianity, but in the fourth century the Emperor Constantine made it the official religion of the Empire. After the fall of the Empire Christianity was not wiped out. Even though the invading tribes were not Christians nearly all of them converted to Christianity very soon after invading. Rome continued to be the centre of the church, and even today, the Pope still lives in Rome and is head of the 'Roman Catholic Church'.

Buildings

For many people the most impressive legacy of the Romans can be seen not in art or literature, but in their magnificent buildings. No visitor to Rome can fail to be impressed by the Colosseum and all over the world there is evidence of the skill of the Romans as architects and builders. The Romans built huge aqueducts to carry water, a massive wall 177 km long in Britain and sewers, bath houses and central heating in their own villas. When the Roman Empire collapsed many of these building skills were lost. In Britain, for example, it was to be over a thousand years before the road system returned to the standards the Romans had set.

Conclusion

For over six hundred years the Romans dominated most of the world which lay in or near to Europe. However, it is also true that there were millions of people throughout the world who never saw a Roman, because Roman influence never extended to places such as South America and Japan. Those countries that were in the Roman Empire benefited from the Romans' skills in areas such as warfare, engineering and government. When the Empire fell in those areas, mankind took a step backwards. There were some Roman practices, such as slavery and the appalling cruelty of the Games, which were less of a loss to the world. But there can be no doubt that, in this country, although the Romans might be gone, they are not forgotten.

Source B

The Arc de Triomphe in Paris. It was built in the early nineteenth century to commemorate the victories of the great French general Napoleon.

Titus

Titus was born in AD 39. He became emperor when his father, Vespasian, died in AD 79. He was a good soldier and won many battles. The Arch of Titus (Source A) celebrates one of these.

Titus is also famous for finishing the Colosseum (see Source B, page 4), a huge arena begun by his father, Vespasian.

amphitheatre a round unroofed building with rows of seats surrounding an arena.

archaeologists experts who study the remains of ancient civilizations that are buried in the earth.

artefacts everyday objects.

auxiliaries foreign troops used to fight for a country at war.

centuries the smallest band of soldiers in the Roman army consisting of 80–100 men.

chain-mail armour made of metal rings linked together.

cohort a group of six **centuries** (480–600) men, in the Roman army.

drill training in military exercises.

excavation the digging of trenches in the ground to uncover ancient remains.

faeces waste matter from the body.

fortified a place or building strengthened against attack with walls or ditches.

hypocaust under-floor heating system.

Legacy of Rome the Roman influence on life throughout the Empire that remained for centuries: e.g. Roman roads, buildings, language, literature and art.

legate soldier in command of a legion.

legion the largest division of the Roman Army, (5000 men, 10 cohorts).

manoeuvres large-scale exercises of troops.

merchants traders who bought and sold goods with foreign countries.

mineralised changed slowly into a mineral over a long period of time.

mosaics patterns made by placing together small pieces of coloured glass or stone.

province lands in one country ruled by another country.

Renaissance the revival during the 15th and 16th centuries of classical art and learning.

republic a state run by elected representatives of the people.

scabbard a sheath (case) for a sword.

settlement a group of houses like a small village.

slingers soldiers who hurled stones at the enemy with slings.

Specia family gods. Every Roman family worshipped their own household gods who, they believed, would protect them throughout life.

standard flag or carving carried on a long pole by the standard bearer – an important soldier – to inspire the soldiers to follow him into battle.

tenants farmers and workers who rented land or buildings from the owners of country villas.

trident three-pronged spear.

vallum walls and ditches built as a defence.

visor hinged shield attached to a helmet to protect the eyes.